SHE'S GONE BRIDAL!

SHE'S GONE BRIDAL!

A 9-Step Program for Dealing with Your Bride from Hell

LIZ RAZIN

CITADEL PRESS
Kensington Publishing Corp.
www.kensingtonbooks.com

CITADEL PRESS BOOKS are published by

Kensington Publishing Corp.
850 Third Avenue
New York, NY 10022

All Kensington titles, imprints, and distributed lines are available at special quantity discounts for bulk purchases for sales promotions, premiums, fund-raising, educational, or institutional use. Special book excerpts or customized printings can also be created to fit specific needs. For details, write or phone the office of the Kensington special sales manager: Kensington Publishing Corp., 850 Third Avenue, New York, NY 10022, attn: Special Sales Department; phone 1-800-221-2647.

CITADEL PRESS and the Citadel logo are Reg. U.S. Pat. & TM Off.

First printing: April 2009

10 9 8 7 6 5 4 3 2 1

Printed in the United States of America

Library of Congress Control Number: 2008942170

ISBN-13: 978-0-8065-2939-4
ISBN-10: 0-8065-2939-3

To Edgar and Mildred:

I started writing because of you.
Now I'll never stop thanks to you.

Contents

Acknowledgments

M om, there are not enough words in this book to express my gratitude. Thank you for your tireless love, wisdom, and eagle-like editor's eye. Whether you were clipping wedding articles or brainstorming gentler alternatives to the word "Bridezilla," I treasure every moment you devoted to this book.

Dad, who could have been more perfect to learn from than you? A real-life therapist who not only loves what he does but excels at it every day. Thank you for teaching me how to be my own version of a therapist—even without the PhD.

Mike, my lovable human thesaurus, thank you for constantly providing the perfect pop culture reference and for coping with my inability to multi-task. I am lucky that you were always there with enthusiasm and humor, even when *I* was the one who needed therapy.

Lauren Abramo, my agent, I am forever grateful for your kindness, gentleness and insight—everything a first-time author wishes for. Thank you for finding the right home for *She's Gone Bridal!*

Danielle Chiotti, you are the world's most down-to-earth and supportive editor—and now "mommy"—who took a risk with this Personal Bridal Therapist. Thank you for filling every conversation and editorial comment with respect, thoughtfulness and spirit.

Amy Pyle, thank you for your editorial guidance and grace.

Maia Dunkel, author and friend, I truly value how you graciously taught me the basics and so much more about the industry.

ACKNOWLEDGMENTS

All the wonderful women who shared their inspiring wedding stories with me and continuously asked, "So, how's the book?"— Katie Razin, Michelle Mulroe, Jill Fink, Suzanne Hereghty, Dorianne Coventry, Lindsey Letteri, Meridith Piper, Anne Goldfield, Julie Dombreval, Mary Carmen Gasco-Buisson, Amy Starkman, Mariana Dimitrova, Heather Dominiak, Lindsey Randolph, Tiffany Flomo, Suzanne Ayello, Beverly Okada.

SHE'S GONE
BRIDAL!

Getting Started

When she's the one getting married,
why are you the one saying "I do"
to wedding agony?

The First Question Any Good Therapist Asks:
Why Are You Here?

Y ou read the title, *She's Gone Bridal!* Instantly, you thought of the bride in your life, perhaps your best friend. The one you've known since third grade. The one who's making you wear that dreadful sapphire monster of a dress to her wedding in June.

Then you thought of your cousin and how you've secretly nick-named her "Brat-to-Be," but call her "The Beautiful Bride" to her face.

Maybe you thought of your friend Courtney from work who refuses to conduct any form of business beyond selecting the perfect wedding invitations and writing somewhat heartfelt vows. She's the one who starts every status meeting with a mandatory count-down to her wedding day. She's the one who pretends to take copious notes during meetings, but who is actually writing out all the possible ways she can take his last name: "Ms. Courtney Jones . . . Mrs. Courtney Franklin-Jones . . . Mrs. C. Jones . . . Ms. Jones."

Perhaps you thought of your friend from softball camp who e-mails you every other day with pictures of her perfectly man-icured hand—yes, her hand! The hand that used to be covered with a worn-in catcher's mitt. The hand that is *now* adorned with a new emerald cut DeBeers engagement ring she waited four years for.

Or maybe someone gave you this book as a gift. Someone who knows what you've *really* gone through lately. Someone who knows that you've spent just about every weekend in the past two years at a wedding, an engagement party, or a bridal shower or that you were lucky enough to have spent your very last Sky Mile on yet *another* Vegas bachelorette party that proved, once again, "what happens in Vegas . . ." isn't always so great.

Perhaps it was someone who knows that your cat no longer recognizes you when you come home from one of your trips to the world's most exotic wedding hot spots, like Bada-Bing-filled Bayonne, New Jersey, or frigid Minneapolis, Minnesota.

It could be someone who knows that you have a balance of negative $26 in your bank account, having spent your last dime—and then some—on the perfect tea set that you chose from your college roommate's Crate & Barrel wedding registry. Or that you went into overdraft for those must-have alterations to the turquoise bridesmaid number your sister declared "needs to be tea length!" for her spring reception.

Only someone who knows the cold, hard bridal truth about your life would give you this book. Only someone who knows that the most important person in your life right now is no longer you. *Somehow,* it is a Bride to Be (BTB)!

No matter *how* this book landed in your hands, it could not have come at a better time. No matter who you are, no matter where you live, no matter how old you are, or no matter how many weddings you have been to, there is a bond that unites every reader of this book. It is a bond that cannot be broken by even the strongest of the bridal species.

There's a bride in your life. And she's driving you crazy!

Just Promise Me This!

Before we get started, all I ask of you is two things:

1. Memorize the following statements: "Yes, of course seafoam green is my favorite color." "No, I don't mind spending time with your sweaty cousin Jerry." And "Of course you're not being unreasonable. This is *your* wedding."

2. Prepare to journey through the nine stages of bridal anguish described in this guide.

Take these two things to heart and, I promise, you will survive. And maybe, one of the thousands of times you force a smile at your bride, you will actually feel true joy. Well, maybe not.

Yours truly,
Your Personal Bridal Therapist (PBT)

CHAPTER ONE

Stage I: Denial

Admitting you have a problem,
a bridal *problem!*

You Need Therapy—*Bridal* Therapy, That Is

Freud. Erikson. Maslow. All important therapists in their own right. But did any of *them* ever encounter a woman in the same state of bridal desperation as you? Someone who needs the kind of help you do to cope with your bride? Someone living in the same wicked world of weddings that you do?

I think not!

In your case, no ordinary therapist will do, only someone who has RSVPed to far too many wedding receptions, someone who has struggled to fit into way too many hideous bridesmaid dresses, including the one that needed to be reordered in the next size (who knew I'd be addicted to Taco Bell that winter?), or someone who has felt the wrath of many a Bride from Hell.

Only a Personal Bride Therapist (PBT) who is expertly trained in the art and science of Bridal Therapy will do.

"What is Bridal Therapy?" you ask. Well, my nuptially challenged friend, Bridal Therapy is the first therapy designed specifically with you—the victim of the bride—in mind. It puts the bride aside for once and for all, arming *you* with the lifesaving tips, case studies, and easy-to-learn techniques you need to survive—and thrive—in this wedding-infested world.

In fact, by the time you finish reading this book, you'll be chanting, "Bring it on, bride!"

What the Heck Is a Personal Bridal Therapist, Anyhow?

Having been a bridesmaid more times than I can count on my non-Tiffany ring-wearing hand and having attended nearly every wedding on the entire East Coast of the United States, I can safely say that I have experienced far more than my fair share of weddings.

I have padded more brides' bras than I can remember so that they could perfectly fill out their Vera Wangs.

I have agonized over finding the absolutely *perfect* wedding gift. And I have still wondered afterward: "Does she really use the professional-grade cappuccino maker that I blew last year's bonus on?"

I have held many a bride's hair back while she puked her brains out at her bachelorette party.

I have even danced two—count 'em, two—slow songs with creepy Uncle Norton so that he would stop hitting on my bride. To this day, the smell of his brandy-infused breath still haunts me. Eww!

I have survived the good, the bad, the ugly—and I mean *really* ugly—brides of the world. I have seen brides cry. I have heard brides scream. I have seen a few of 'em gaze—terrified—down that long aisle like a deer caught in headlights. I've even seen one completely lose it when her cellulite-reduction pantyhose split right down her leg as she was lifted in the air to dance the Hora.

But most important—for you—I have seen and felt firsthand how oblivious brides can be about the havoc they wreak on the lives of those closest to them. Those of us left to fend for ourselves.

As your PBT, I vow to be there—even when your bride isn't—to help you survive any wedding with finesse.

The Rules of Bridal Therapy

As you enter the first stage of Bridal Therapy, Stage I, let's establish some guiding principles for your treatment program.

Bridal Therapy Rule #1: Just because you're *not a* bride, doesn't mean you're not worth it.

This is a crucial rule in Bridal Therapy. Playing second fiddle to the bride so frequently, you may forget that you, too, are important. But just because you're not falling over from the weight of a mammoth ring doesn't mean you don't deserve happiness. In fact, this book will help you recreate it.

Bridal Therapy Rule #2: You're in the safe "wedding-free" zone.

It may be hard to "turn off" wedding mode once you're in the thick of it, but think of our time together as "wedding-free" time.

This is *your* time to focus on you—and only you—and to regain your self-assurance, strength, and sense of self. When you're in the wedding-free zone, *you* take priority. Period.

Bridal Therapy Rule #3: Talk the talk.

There are a few bridal abbreviations that we'll use throughout this book. Take a look.

- BFF = Best Friend Forever
- BLB = Bride–Life Balance
- BM = It stands for Bridesmaid, silly.
- BTB = Bride to Be

- MOB = Mother of the Bride
- MOH = Maid of Honor
- PBT = Personal Bridal Therapist (that's me!)
- TMBI = Too Much Bridal Information. Just like TMI, but with a bride to boot!
- WW = Wedding Withdrawal

Now that you've learned the rules of Bridal Therapy, you're truly ready to tackle Stage I!

Is My Best Friend Forever Really Marrying *That* Guy?

In some cases, you've known "him" for years. You've seen him in his smiley face boxers as he's scurried out of the bathroom. You've even heard him having sex with your best friend in the next room of your Miami share.

You know the dosage of his Propecia, the dimensions of his right bicep, the amount of money he dropped on roses for Valentine's Day, and the number of times he's cried in front of her.

He's the "I know more about him than my *own* boyfriend" boyfriend.

In other cases, you don't know much about him at all—only that he's *suddenly* the most important thing in her life.

Meet the "Who the hell is this guy? And what has he done with my BFF?" boyfriend. All you know is that your Best Friend Forever (BFF) was once a take-charge, independent woman who worked eighteen hours a day as a copywriter and—with the blink of an eye—this stranger took over her world.

To make matters worse, sometimes, odd little tidbits pop out of the mouth of the "Who the hell is this guy? And what has he done with my BFF?" boyfriend. Like he enjoys visiting rundown insane asylums in Vermont or he decorates his bedroom with *Star Wars* figures in their original packaging.

Then there is the "bad news" boyfriend. All you know about this guy is, well, nothing good. You know about the time he pinched another girl's butt at a party. You know he prefers Burger King fries to McDonald's fries—normally a great point, but not if he *works* at Burger King. And you know he wears more jewelry on one hand than she wears on her entire body.

No matter which profile best suits him, when your bride's personal call comes in from her Greece getaway at 2:00 A.M. or the "Urgent" group e-mail shows up in your inbox at work, the news will rock you to the core. Inevitably, an overwhelming sense of shock comes along with the announcement that your BFF or sister or cousin or co-worker will actually be spending the rest of her life with this guy. And along with shock, comes a flurry of questions.

How could she? Aren't you supposed to spend the rest of your lives ravaging bars until 5:00 A.M.? Wasn't it yesterday when she declared she would be your "Wing Woman" forever?

Isn't she too young? Wasn't she just in braces? Doesn't she still have a crush on Jon Stewart?

What happened to her feminist ideals? Did she just introduce herself with *his* last name? Has the excitement of marriage clouded her $150,000 Stanford-educated brain?

Is he the right guy? Why couldn't she just find a nice day trader? You swore she mentioned that idea when you were in college. Wait, maybe that was *your* idea.

Your PBT Says: Test Your *Bridal Mode* Skills

No matter how many questions pop into your head when you get the news that your friend is getting married, you must default immediately to Bridal Mode. Remember this term, as you will need to use it many times throughout your voyage. Bridal Mode basically means to smile hard, tear up, and say only good things.

Do whatever you need to do to convey elation and love—even though what you really feel is sick to your stomach. Let out a giant scream, hug her tightly, or put 10,000 exclamation points after the "Congratulations" in your response e-mail.

Take Alexis J., age 26—the personification of Bridal Mode.

Bridal Case File #41: Alexis J.

Alexis J. was the coolest, calmest, and most accommodating friend of a bride you could imagine. When her bride asked her to take a five-hour trip to Napa Valley just to taste the $32-a-glass Merlot for the rehearsal dinner, Alexis J. was there. When her bride sobbed over the "disastrous" teal lining of her satin heels, Alexis J. hand delivered a pair of Dr. Scholl's.

But while Alexis J.'s bride was going crazy over wine choices and lining colors, Alexis J. was going crazy over her breakup with her boyfriend of two years. In fact, the night Alexis J.'s boyfriend broke her heart, Alexis J.'s bride made her final picks for the bridal party. When her bride called her an hour after the painful breakup, Alexis J. exclaimed, "I'm so glad that you called."

"Me too!" screamed her bride. "Will you be my Maid of Honor?"

Alexis J. instinctively sprang into Bridal Mode. With the poise of Jackie-O, she told her bride, "Of course! This is a dream come true—knowing that you've found the man you'll spend the rest of your life with and that I'll be there to witness it all!"

Of course, Alexis J. shared her *own* news with her bride

the next day. And by constantly using her champion Bridal Mode skills, Alexis J. got through the tough time with her pride intact.

Here are some other Bridal Mode responses to the engagement news:

+ I am so incredibly happy for you guys!
+ I've met many, many of your boyfriends, but I knew he was the one!
+ Nothing makes me happier than knowing that the two of you will be together forever!

Feel free to personalize and tweak these statements. But don't stray too far. Remember, convey elation and love—and you can't go wrong, even if *she's* gone wrong with that Burger King baboon.

Your PBT Says: Take 24 and Call Me in the Morning

Before you launch into full Bridal Mode, give yourself twenty-four hours to let the engagement news sink in. Allow yourself time to ask the tormenting questions that continually surface as you lie in bed watching Conan or ride the subway train half-asleep.

+ Yes, you will find someone for yourself.
+ Yes, he will be handsome. He will take care of you and remember the important things about you, like the fact that you like Dannon Light yogurt in strawberries and banana—not mixed berry.

- No, you are not the only person on the planet who is yet to be engaged. You may be the only person in your circle of friends, but certainly not the entire planet.

- No, you are not the most insecure person in the world. Sure, you feel more insecure at twenty-nine than you did giving your "Vote for Me" speech when you ran for class president fourteen years ago. But you are not *the* most insecure person in the world.

Whatever answers make you feel slightly better about yourself win! Remember the winners. Write them down on post-its and stick 'em on the fridge. Save one as your screensaver at work. Make one the mantra you silently chant whenever you feel the "Bridal Blues." It will help, I swear.

Your PBT Says: Take the News to Heart—or to Stomach

It is one thing to tell the bride how happy you are for her and to jump up and down with forced glee. It is another to grasp that this is *really* happening—she is really getting married. Not to fret! During the Denial Phase, you can do many things to help digest this stomach-turning engagement news:

- Don't hug it out. Write it out. Try soaking up your sadness by writing a heartfelt card to the bride and hubby to be. A personal note saying, "Congratulations to my two favorite people," is code for: "I accept you, Fiancé Man. And, I forgive you for getting married, Bride."

- Spend money. Another way to make the news stick is to send the bride and her fiancé an engagement gift. Spending money will quickly help you realize that, yes, she is engaged. And, yes, you are spending $139 on a Pottery Barn Barista Coffee Set.

♦ Tell your parents. This forces you to deal with your worst nightmare head-on. No matter how strong your relationship with your parents, many of us may wonder, "Are my parents sitting at home counting down the days until their precious daughter gets married?"

In most cases, your parents have tons of other stuff to worry about, like when they'll be able to catch up on "Deal or No Deal." But it may help you feel better to alert them to your BFF's bridal news.

If, once you break the news, they ask—or hint at—when it will be *your* turn, respond with the composure you know how to muster up with Bridal Mode: "I promise, you will be the first people I call as soon as it happens."

Bridal Case File #6: Susie F.

You can also do as Susie F. did: manage the unmanageable mom.

By the time Susie F. turned twenty-seven, all four of her closest girlfriends from Emory were engaged. And while Susie F. had a few semi-suitable suitors up her sleeve, she was nowhere near getting engaged, nor did she want to be.

When her twin sister broke the earth-shattering news over Thanksgiving dinner that she, too, would be joining the "Engagement Club," the news settled just fine into Susie F.'s already turkey-filled stomach. The problem: it didn't sit so well with Susie F.'s overly involved and eager-to-see-her-daughter-marry-rich mother. After congratulating the "good" twin, Susie F.'s mother grabbed her hand and told Susie F.

just loudly enough for everyone at the table to hear her, "Don't worry, Suze, we'll find a husband for you soon."

Susie F.'s response was textbook Bridal Mode. Rather than running off sobbing, she simply told her, "Don't worry, Mom. The longer I wait, the bigger the diamond!" That kept her mom quiet for the next couple of months.

Your PBT Says: Take the Test

The flurry of engagement news has died down. You've come out of your room for the first time in a week. You've stopped eating Edy's Rocky Road twice a day. You've faced your worst nightmare — her engagement — with charm and self-assuredness. You fully realize that your best friend, your beloved sister, or your favorite cousin is a new breed of woman — a bride. Or at least you think you have.

The fact is, even though you may have acknowledged that she is engaged, you may not have truly *internalized* that she's engaged. What's the key to determining whether you've truly accepted that she's a BTB? The foolproof, time-tested Bridal Denial Test. Read on for more details.

Bridal Denial Test Directions

1. Read each of the statements that follows.

2. Choose an answer without giving it too much thought and circle either *T* for true or *F* for false next to each statement. Remember, this is therapy for your sake and no one else's, so be honest.

3. Count the number of *T*s and *F*s.

Bridal Denial Test Questions

1. You've attempted to set your BTB up on two blind dates since she's announced her engagement. T F

2. You can't seem to understand why she's suddenly stopped making out with random guys at your favorite dive bar. T F

3. You still haven't bought her an engagement gift, and it's been eight months since the engagement announcement. T F

4. You still look at pictures of the two of you from that "singles-only" booze cruise in Mexico, and you say to yourself, "I'm so glad nothing has changed." T F

5. You haven't put her wedding date into your BlackBerry calendar. T F

6. You've caught yourself making jokes about her being a "wild and crazy" single woman more than four times this week. T F

7. You can't seem to remember her fiancé's name. Harry? Harvey? Hillbilly? T F

8. You haven't told your parents that she's engaged. T F

9. You showed up over two hours late to her engagement party and couldn't understand why she was upset that you missed the big toast. T F

10. You still refer to her fiancé as "her latest hook up" or "boy toy." T F

11. You continue to introduce her as "my favorite *single* friend." T F

12. You worked for two hours to get the two of you on "the list" of your favorite club for Friday's "singles" night. T F

13. You see her engagement ring and wonder, "When is she going to give this loaner back to Tiffany's?" T F

Bridal Denial Test Scoring System

11+ *T*s: You're in serious denial.

7–10 *T*s: You need a bit of a reality check.

4–6 *T*s: You're on your way to acceptance.

1–3 *T*s: You've truly accepted the news.

Your PBT Says: Do Your Darnedest to Defeat Denial

No matter your score, you've come to the right place for recovery, my darling. Your PBT will help you overcome even the worst case of "Bridal Denial."

The first step? Understanding denial. So, let's turn to our friend Anna Freud. That's right. She's Sigmund Freud's darling daughter who defined denial as a defense mechanism used when someone is faced with a fact that is too difficult to deal with.

"Enough psychobabble! Break it down for me, PBT," you must be saying. In layman's—or laywoman's—bridal terms, Freud is telling us that denial is just a fancy word for a front we put up when we are faced with a fact that is too painful to accept. It is so horrible that, instead of dealing with it, we reject the idea entirely and tell ourselves it is not true.

Bridal Case File #12: Julie P.

Meet Julie P. If you thought *you* were in denial, just wait till you hear her denial story.

Julie P. happened to be on a lovely family vacation on the lake when her BFF called with the "best news ever!"

One sunny afternoon at the beach, just as Julie P. was preparing to flip over to bronze her backside, her cell phone rang. She knew from the cheesy Fergie ringtone who it was without looking at the phone.

"Hi babe," Julie P. said and sighed as relaxed as could be.

In contrast, her best friend on the other end was breathless with excitement. You could actually hear her panting over the newly polished sparkler on her left hand. "Jason just proposed to me! We're getting married!"

Perhaps Julie P. was a tad dehydrated from the hours she'd spent in the sun that week. Maybe the sunblock had clouded her eyes. No matter what it was exactly, the biggest thing ever to happen to her best friend just didn't seem like that big of a deal to Julie P.

"That's such great news. I'm so excited," Julie P. told her best friend without much effort. It was as if Julie P. had just heard that her best friend bought a cute dress on sale or found out what time *The Hills* was going to be on next season. No biggie.

Julie P.'s "no biggie" attitude continued for months—even as she attended her best friend's engagement party and spent hours trying on bridesmaid dresses. For some reason, the "bigness" of the news just did not sink in. It was not until the morning of the wedding that Julie P. broke out of her denial.

Julie P. woke up with the absolute worst stomachache in the world and assumed it was from the four shots of Patrone from the night before. When she realized that her stomachache was not from the alcohol, but rather from butterflies, she told her fellow bridesmaid, "I guess I'm just a little emotional about today."

When her fellow bridesmaid responded, "What are *you* so upset about?" Julie P.'s response shot out of her mouth as if it had been held captive inside for years. "Maybe it's the fact that my best friend in the whole wide world is leaving me to marry this crazy guy who I've only spent a total of forty-five minutes with. Maybe—just maybe—it's that things are never, ever going to be the same again!"

When she finished her rant, Julie P. realized that tears were streaming down her face, destroying the Trish McEvoy makeup she just paid seventy-five bucks for, and that the five other bridesmaids were staring at her.

So, my patient, what can you learn from Julie P.? That it's very important to tackle any feelings of denial up front. You don't want to ruin your eye makeup the day of the wedding, now do you?

Now that Julie P. has illustrated a bit more about denial, *you're* ready to beat it. The masterful tactics in the pages ahead, inspired by real-life therapies, are guaranteed to have you introducing your BFF/sister/cousin as a BTB in no time.

Denial Tactic 1: Know the rules of the wedding game.

No one likes being kept in the dark. Some brides may *look* as if they got dressed in the dark. But, seriously, knowing what to expect for the next few months as your BTB prepares to marry can ease the blow of Stage I. Here are the three unofficial tips to dealing with your bride—including the *unofficial* ones Martha Stewart wouldn't dare tell you:

♦ *Rule #1: Your life is about to change.* Forget about money—all disposable income will now be used for bridal purposes only. Forget about freedom—all the spare time you used to spend searching match.com or eharmony.com will be spent searching for the perfect, white feather pen for her guestbook.

+ *Rule #2: You are officially "on call" at all times.* That's right. As her friend or relative, your bride has unspokenly told you, "Be at my beck and call at all times."
+ *Rule #3: Your new job title is "party planner, CEO."* You're likely going to be responsible for helping to plan, pay for, and attend the wedding shower and the bachelorette party. You'll find more specific tips on these oh-so-fun events in Stage VI.

Denial Tactic 2: Say it loud. Say it proud.

One of the easiest ways to accept that she's getting married is to say "She's getting married" out loud. Sounds simple, right? But for those of us in deep denial, uttering those words ain't always so easy. Nonetheless, doing so can make a big difference.

Start slowly by writing this phrase down on a piece of paper. Write your friend's name—and no substituting Daffy Duck or Jessica Rabbit. Then complete the sentence with "is getting married."

Read the sentence to yourself three times. When you're ready, upgrade to a whisper. And when you're feeling a bit cocky, say it out loud at normal speaking volume.

Once you've said it out loud in a room by yourself, you're ready to try it on other humans. Give it a whirl with folks you don't care that much about it—perhaps an acquaintance at work or friend at a bar. Then, move on to your mother or your college friends.

Repeat at least five times and you're golden. In this case, perhaps you're platinum!

Denial Tactic 3: Desensitize, darling.

Desensitization is a powerful, real-life technique that harnesses the power of your imagination to overcome denial. As you might imagine, desensitization does just what it sounds like: it desensitizes you to the problem. The magic ingredient? Make believe.

Start by taking a seat. Find a comfy recliner if possible. If not, that seat next to the drunken guy on the El will have to do. Then, close your eyes. Okay, so that's hard to do while you're reading, but give it a try. You're resourceful.

Now ask yourself, "How will your bride's wedding dress look on the big day?"

In most cases, the thought of your bride on the "big day" in her "big dress" is so scary that your brain cannot fathom the idea.

But don't avoid the question or answer with your usual sarcasm. As hard as it is to imagine, really think about it. Hear the wedding bells chime and the music play in the church. Feel the petals of soft flowers in the perfectly created bouquets. Smell the slightly offensive cologne of the groomsmen. And now there she is. Your BTB. She's smiling. She's glowing. She's so happy.

Do you have a mental picture of her? Now describe the dress. Is it white? Is it cream? Is the fabric shiny or matte? Is it lace or velvet? Is the neck sweetheart or halter? Is the length tea or floor length? Imagine every detail from coifed head to manicured toe.

Now open your eyes.

Are you smiling? Hopefully.

And guess what? You've officially conquered your worst fear—imagining your bride living happily ever after—at least on her wedding day. And now that you've experienced this idea in your imagination, you can take it on in real life.

Congratulations—you've officially been desensitized!

And for those rare cases in which this desensitization technique does not work, have no fear, my bridal friend. Your PBT's got other proven Denial Tactics up her psychological sleeve! Just keep on truckin'.

Denial Tactic 4: Accept responsibility.

"What? Accept responsibility for *her* engagement?" you ask. "Her engagement is not my fault!" you say. "It's that funny-looking fiancé man who's responsible for this horror. Not me!"

That's where you're wrong. Just as someone overcoming an addiction needs to accept responsibility for her problem, you need to accept the fact that you—either directly or indirectly—have helped set your bride on this path toward matrimony.

If you honestly answer yes to one or more of these questions, then yes, indeed, you are somehow responsible:

1. You set them up on their first date. Y N

2. You told her he was "soooo dreamy." Y N

3. You helped him pick out the ring. Y N

4. You double dated with your BTB and her fiancé. Y N

5. You told her you really liked him—whether or not you actually did. Y N

See what I mean? Even if you didn't actually introduce them or push him to "pop the question," your actions have somehow contributed to this engagement. Now suck it up and take some credit for it.

Once you see yourself as contributing to this event, it's pretty hard to stay in denial. You'll see.

Denial Tactic 5: You grieve, girl!

The American Handbook of Psychiatry defines *grief* as "the normal response to the loss of a loved one." In this bridal situation, you're mourning her loss in a slightly different way. You're mourning the loss of the fun-lovin' single person she once was. The crazy, wild child you'd give anything—even your new Miu Miu sandals—to spend one last night on the town with.

The secret formula for successfully grieving your no-longer-single friend is the 1 + 1 = 3 technique.

Okay, so the math doesn't work out exactly right. I said I was a therapist, not Einstein!

In this case, when the two pieces are added together, the whole is greater than the sum of its parts. Make sense? Let's try it out:

Let's tackle the first 1. Think of your fondest memory with your bride. Maybe the time you went bowling in sixth grade and her scrunched-down neon socks got caught in her bowling shoes as she catapulted herself down the bowling lane. Or perhaps the time your sister pretended she didn't like that boy from basketball camp so that you could go after him. Maybe the Christmas break that you spent in Vermont with your cousin selling personally tie-dyed Dead T-shirts.

Spend about 30 seconds thinking about this memory. Ask yourself, "How does this make me feel?"

Now, let's move on to the second 1. In this case, it represents another memory of your time together over a lovely beverage. Maybe it was the Cosmo you downed at that Martini bar downtown or the nasty shots of who knows what from that frat party freshman year or the Bartles & James wine cooler that you stole from your parents' fridge.

Spend another thirty seconds or so thinking about your second 1. Oftentimes, it helps to recreate the drink that you enjoyed together. So pop open that champagne and add a splash of Tropicana. Remember this time, you're drinking Mimosas for one, please.

Now that you have your 1s completed, try adding them together. There is no way these memories only add up to a measly 2. When you put them together, they are far greater! See? Math works in mysterious ways.

Another way to grieve is to spend some time looking through

your old scrapbook, yearbook, vacation pictures, or anything that reminds you of your single life together. Spend a few minutes looking at each item. Remember how you felt and how happy you were.

Whether you used the 1 + 1 = 3 technique or one of your PBT's other delightful Denial Tactics, you should be showing off your pearly whites right about now—complete with a big, denial-free smile!

Your PBT Says: Cure the *Worst* Type of Denial

You may have *thought* that pretending she's not really getting married is as bad as Bridal Denial gets. Not always true.

Sometimes, those of us dealing with the bride demonstrate an even more extreme type of denial: acting out.

This type of denial occurs when you've gone beyond ignoring that she's getting married to wanting the marriage *actually* not to happen altogether. And most often, when you don't want it to happen, you act out—just like a child might do when in an uncomfortable situation.

"The horror!" you say. "I am no child! I want to stop this type of behavior before it even has a chance to start."

To begin to defeat this worst-case scenario form of denial, start by taking the following quiz.

"Am I Acting Out? Test" Directions

1. Read each of the statements under Questions.

2. Choose an answer without giving it too much thought and circle either *T* for true or *F* for false next to each statement.

3. Count the number of *T*s and *F*s.

"Am I Acting Out? Test" Questions

1. You have sent her at least four links to the latest female empowerment movies to hit the big screen. T F

2. You showed up two hours late to her dress fitting. T F

3. You "accidentally" scheduled an important business meeting in China the day after her bridal shower so that you couldn't attend the event. T F

4. You've gained so much weight that you won't be able to fit into your bridesmaid dress. T F

5. You've gotten pregnant, so you *definitely* will not be able to fit into your bridesmaid dress. T F

6. You found out that her boyfriend's name means "devil" in Russian and are happy to tell her. T F

7. You were put in charge of decorations for her bachelorette party and completely flaked. At the last minute, you chose My Little Pony plates and balloons. T F

8. You convinced her to have her wedding outside in January, telling her a little snow never hurt anyone. T F

9. You reminded her fiancé about the time she hooked up with the entire football team in college, just to give *him* second thoughts. T F

10. You reminded her about the time her fiancé kissed that girl in Las Vegas when they were "on a break," just to give *her* second thoughts. T F

"Am I Acting Out? Test" Scoring System

8–10 Ts: You're officially a child.

4–7 Ts: You're a teenager who acts out once in a while.

1–3 Ts: You've got your acting out under control.

Whether you scored an alarming 10 or a more digestible 4 on the quiz, you need to learn how to rein *in* your acting *out*. The secret? Anytime you notice even the smallest sign of fifth-grade behavior, stop and ask yourself, "How old am I really?"

If your answer is a number higher than eighteen, then there's no excuse for your childlike tantrums. Sure, your bride may be a pain in the rear. Sure, she deserves to be put in her bridal place. But you're a bigger, better, more mature woman than that. Don't let your Bride from Hell turn you into that bratty girl from fifth grade who everyone hated!

Your PBT Says: Learn to Play Second Fiddle

Another challenging part of the denial stage is coming to the realization that you are no longer the center of your BTB's world. You are no longer the first person she calls when something tragic happens at work. You are no longer her first choice for a dinner date out on the town.

But that doesn't mean she loves you any less than she did before. It's just that she has someone new in her life who takes priority—sometimes over you—as painful as that may be.

Accepting this early on is key to overcoming denial, and most importantly, keeping your ego firmly intact. Here are a few signs that it is time to accept that her fiancé, Chad, is now the most important person in her life—not you.

1. She *somehow* forgot to tell you about her new promotion.

2. She replaced the picture on her fridge—circa 1999—of the two of you at Spring Break in Cancun with a picture of the happy couple.

3. She describes her "chilling out" plans for the evening as ordering in and catching up on her TiVo-ed shows, but you're no longer invited.

4. She has officially replaced you as her "gym buddy" with her fiancé.

5. He's officially "there" whenever you call her.

6. She's no longer available to hang out with you alone—you are always the third wheel.

But just because he takes on a new priority in her life does not mean that you are no longer important to her. It just takes a little getting used to. In fact, your relationship has probably already changed somewhat since they have been dating. So being second in line should not come as a huge shock to you.

In some cases, however, she goes beyond making you "second in line" to erasing you from her life: when she goes beyond taking a day to call you back to not calling you back altogether, and when she not only holds his hand for the entire time at the party but says only two words to you.

In this instance, consider sitting down with your bride and letting her know that you miss spending time with her. Acknowledge that she is very busy planning the wedding but that you'd like the two of you to make more of an effort to spend quality time together. Suggest a one-on-one dinner night once a month or taking a yoga class together. These "only the two of us" events can make all the difference.

Your PBT Says: Now That You're Done with Denial, It's Time to Be Nice

As you victoriously dash through the denial stage, it's time to take a moment to reflect on someone other than yourself—the bride. I know, the last person you want to be nice to right now is that evil bridal stepsister who just slid the "let's be single forever" glass slipper out from under you.

But try as best you can to turn your negative feelings into positive energy—even if being positive feels extremely fake in the end, you'll feel proud that you were strong enough to be a good friend.

- A couple of days after the engagement announcement, give her the "That's what friends are for" speech. Let her know that you will be there for her throughout the entire process no matter what.
- Pick one day out of the week, like Wednesday. Rename it "Wedding Wednesday"—your day to call her every week and check in. Mark your calendar with wedding bells, broken hearts, or even skulls. Whatever works for you.

Your PBT Says: Give Yourself a Hug!

Congratulations—you've made it through Stage I! Take pride in knowing that you've made it through the most difficult stage. Well, maybe not the *most* difficult, but one of 'em. Give yourself a hug, or preferably, ask the cute tech guy who works in the cube next to you for a harmless little hug. He doesn't have to know why.

CHAPTER TWO

Stage II: Diagnosis

*How to spot the signs
of Bridezilla behavior*

S he's been your best friend since second grade. You've seen her with crimped hair and big bangs—the first *and* second time they were in.

She was the little sister you bathed with until you were six and traded Jem and the Hologram dolls with until you were twelve.

She was the college roommate you carried home from frat houses freshman year, took to the hospital when she thought she had an STD, and cried with when her grandmother died.

She reflects a bit of who you are today. Maybe who you used to be. Even who you wish you could be in the future.

But no matter who she *used* to be, now she is a BTB. From the moment she says, "Yes, I will marry you," she enters into an alternate universe. Experts call it the "Bridal Dimension"—where logic is forgotten and cake toppers rule.

Worst of all, brides are often blissfully blind to the pain and suffering others must endure when dealing with their new bridal personality.

This chapter is guaranteed to help. It teaches you how to handle even the worst-behaved woman to be wed. The key? Diagnosing her with the correct bridal personality.

You must be saying, "PBT, only an expert such as yourself has the trained eye for such difficult work."

Not true, my bridal jewel! You, too, will quickly learn the tricks of the trade needed to diagnose the worst of 'em faster than she can say, "Where's my blue lace garter belt?"

Your PBT Says: Untap the Unique Psychology of Your Bride

Taking a cue from a Freud yet again, think back to psychology class. You remember *that* class—the only 8:00 A.M. class you woke up for just so you could catch a glimpse of the cute grad-school assistant in his Dockers and worn-down loafers.

Now forget about his perfect apple butt for a moment (I know it's difficult), and remember what Sigmund taught us: he hypothesized that the human psyche is divided into three distinct parts— the id, the ego, and the superego.

The id is trapped way down inside our unconscious; it reflects our hopes, dreams, wishes, and sexual urges. Even those we do not realize exist, like that subconscious crush you still have on James Van Der Beek.

The ego is the go-between the id and reality; it is our most conscious state. It is who we are on the surface—the face we put forward to others every day.

And then there is the superego, our internal system of morals gleaned from our parents and society; it tells us what is wrong and what is right. Think angel on one shoulder and devil on the other.

What Freud did not realize when he created this nearly perfect personality trifecta was that brides actually have a fourth personality dimension: the *brid*. Yes, my clever bridal student, the brid is a combination of the word "bride" and "id." You smarty-pants, you!

And the brid is just what you'd imagine it would be. It is a bride's deep-rooted, unconscious drive to be the world's most perfect bride at the world's most perfect wedding. And because the dreaded brid is trapped deep down in her soul—like the id—the brid does not always surface in the most obvious ways. In fact, most brides are not even aware of their brid. But lucky for you, you soon will be!

Read on to learn more about how the burdensome brid can emerge when you're least expecting it.

Bridal Case File #2: Sofie K.

Sofie K., age 32, had been the absolute perfect matron of honor to her younger cousin from Texas. She drove to Dallas to attend all four of the bride's dress fittings. Yes, I said four! She negotiated day rates with Dallas' premier wedding planner and even haggled with the tailor for a better deal on altering all ten of the bridesmaid dresses. Yes, I said ten! After all, the bride was a very popular Delta Delta back in the day.

For the most part, Sofie K.'s bridal kindness had paid off. Her bride remained cool, calm, and appreciative of all of Sofie K.'s generous wedding assistance. At least until the bride's brid made an unexpected appearance at the rehearsal dinner.

All ninety-four of the out-of-town guests had gathered at Dallas's finest bistro for what *should* have been a night of laughter and celebration. Instead, it became a night of embarrassment for Sofie K.—thanks to the brid.

Several of the couple's friends and family members made special toasts to the soon to be wed. With every toast, the bride took it upon herself to suck down a full—yes, full—glass of the restaurant's finest champagne. And of course, the staff was more than happy to continue to pour her a new glass of the $10-a-pop beverage each time her glass even approached empty.

By the time the fourth toast had been made, the bride was pretty tipsy. By the time the ninth toast had been made, the bride was absolutely, positively bridally blitzed—eyes drooped, hair uncharacteristically frazzled, Southern drawl slurred, and inappropriate comments ablaze. In her drunken state, the bride thought it would be a smart idea to stand up in front of the entire room to thank everyone for coming to the event.

At the end of her mighty wobbly toast, she declared, "I'd like to say a special thank you to my cousin, Sofie. Sofie, will you please come up here? Please?" she asked.

Reluctantly, Sofie K. did as her bride commanded.

"Now, look how pretty Sofie looks tonight, y'all!" The bride went on. "It is just too bad that she was so much heavier at her own weddin'," she said, adding in an attempted aside.

Sofie K. looked at her bride with shock. She thought it was the alcohol talking. But it was really the evil brid emerging.

The bride continued babbling, despite the distress on Sofie K.'s face."Oh, I'm just kiddin'. But, seriously, thank goodness I haven't been eatin' like she did—she was a bit of an oinker back then!"

So what lesson can you learn from this sad story from the South? No matter how nice you are to your bride and no matter how many favors she calls in, expect a brid attack at all times.

As you'll no doubt encounter many times throughout your bridal journey, it's critical to keep your cool—no matter how heated the brid makes you feel. "How?" you ask.

A fellow bridesmaid once told me, simply "Count to the Bridal Ten" whenever the brid gets going. She swore, "Whenever my bride started to go crazy, I just closed my eyes and counted to ten. By the time I got to nine and a half, my blood had stopped boiling and I could re-engage in anything the brid brought on!"

Another tip for your curtailing the vicious brid is to remind yourself that the brid is not permanant. That's right. Your bride can only get away with this behavior for so long.

Sure, you'll forgive her for that flip comment she made about your new highlights "looking like Miley Cyrus gone bad." Sure, you'll suck it up—or in—when she commands that you drop six pounds before the wedding. But that's only for now.

The moment she says her "I do's," you'll be able to say, "No, you don't!" to her attitude. So sit tight and remind yourself that your BTB—just like the brid—is a temporary state that will soon come to an overdue end.

Your PBT Says: Every Bride Has a Vision—You Don't Have to Like It, But You Do Have to Respect It

In addition to vigilantly watching out for the vile brid, the next thing you need to know is that every bride—from Toledo to Toronto—has a unique vision for her big day in the spotlight. A vision in which everything has to be "just so." Sometimes the vision is a day of serenity on Lake Placid. Sometimes it is of elegance at the Four Seasons in Beverly Hills. Sometimes it is of utter debauchery at Fenway Park.

Whatever it is—love it or hate it—take it from me, sister, don't go messin' with it. Respect it. Listen to her talk about it. Help her realize it. But do not criticize it, tamper with it, or make any suggestions to tone it down. Even if you truly believe that the swans and ducks flown in from Tampa seem a bit over the top. Remember, it is her vision and her day.

Colleen T. mastered this lesson. Read on to learn from her success.

Bridal Case File #17: **Colleen T.**

Colleen T.'s bride was an art director at a snooty European PR firm specializing in high-fashion clients. The bride normally dressed in the I-wanna-be-couture-but-can't-afford-it uniform—all black all the time, from her Gucci sunglass-adorned head to Tod's flat-wearing toe.

But for her wedding, the BTB had a unique vision she coined "Monochromatic White." From the satin white Badgley Mischka dress to the white linen tablecloths to the exotic white tulips from Holland. The white-fixated bride even took a cue from Diddy and called for "all white attire" instead of black tie.

All white. All the time.

When the bride's vision was finally realized on her wedding day, Colleen T. thought it looked less like a wedding and more like a holding cell run amuck with straight-jacketed patients. But the bride was happy. For her, it was a white wedding wonderland!

In the end, the bride went back to wearing black the very next day at the wedding brunch. But every now and then, she accents her witchlike wardrobe with a white accent of jewelry.

What Colleen T. did so right in this example was to leave the bride's vision alone. Even though she would have loved to see even a *hint* of color at the event, she knew better than to say so.

What can *you* learn from Colleen T.?

No matter how desperate you are to save your bride from her own poor taste—stop. Take a deep breath, and remind yourself, it's not *your* wedding—it's hers.

No matter how you would have rearranged the flowers that looked like your three-year-old cousin could have easily just picked them, no matter how much longer you would have made the inappropriately short bridesmaid dresses, no matter how much less pretentious food you would have selected to replace the French fois gras and Persian beluga, it's her wedding. Let her do with it what she pleases.

Your PBT Says: She's Queen of the World!

Queen Elizabeth, watch out! You've got nothing on the latest BTB. That's because nearly every one of the two-and-a-half-million women who marry each year in the United States believes *she's* the center of the world. And who can blame her? She's got wedding planners catering to her every whim. Saleswomen holding her hair up as she tries on yet *another* gown, and complete strangers gawking over her princess cut stone every chance they get.

For many a bride, this is the first time in her life in which she truly gets to call the shots. She decides when the wedding will be, how many people will attend, where it will take place, what the bridal party will wear, and so on, and so on.

Taking the reins, even if only for a few months, makes your bride feel powerful. It is fun. It is addictive.

This is also the first, and sometimes the last, time in a bride's life when no one dares say no to her. You want *another* layer on your cake? Sure. You want a *bigger* bustle? No problem! You'd like *another* calla lily in your bouquet. You've got it!

Sure, not hearing the word no may eventually increase the wedding budget. But she's probably not thinking about that right now. Your bride is entranced by her newfound power.

So don't be surprised if, during the course of wedding preparations, your bride starts waving to the crowd or blowing kisses to her countrymen. Just know that this power-hungry behavior is only temporary. And don't be surprised if, when someone happens to utter the word *no*, your bride requires a royal translator!

Your PBT Says: Do Diagnose, My Darling

Now that you understand a bit more about the unique psychology of brides, it's finally time to take your diagnosis skills one step further and tailor them to your *specific* bride. That's right. Strap on your stethoscope. Let's play doctor!

To diagnose disorders, doctors have a bag full of tools at their disposal. They draw blood, check pulse rate, listen to the heart, and take an X-ray on occasion. In your case, your tools are your eyes, ears, and heart. In a nutshell, they are your ability and dissect your bride's symptoms.

Before we delve into your bride's specific personality, we need to cleanse you of your negative feelings about the bride. This is your time to create a blank slate—to start fresh and diagnose her objectively—and your chance to not let your own feelings get in the way.

To do so, a bit of Freud's most famous technique, Free Association, is in order:

1. Start by taking out a blank piece of paper.

2. Write down your bride's name.

3. Write down the words that come into your head about

her: nice, mean, funny, sloppy, drunk, bitchy, and so on. Seriously, whatever comes into your head goes on the paper.

4. Continue writing.

5. Wait about three minutes, and you should feel a sense of calm come over you. A sense that all your pent-up anger and frustration has been released.

6. Keep the document—save it, tape it to your fridge, put it in your pocket—but do *not* let your bride read it.

Now that you've released your pent-up personal feelings about your bride from the situation, you are ready to do some *real* diagnosin'! This should be fun.

Your PBT Says: Take Notes on Diagnosing These Terrible Types of Brides

Bridezilla

Brat

My bride

Bitch to Be

Bride from Hell

Slave Driver

I'm sure you have a lot of nicknames for your bride—some less flattering than others. This section will help you go one step beyond nasty nicknames to dissect the particular personality of your bride. Thanks to your PBT's very own Bridal Segmentation Study, you'll learn about each of the individual bridal personalities and then diagnose your bride with the appropriate one. Plus, you'll learn how to survive life with each type of bride with must-have therapies tailored to each personality.

The secret tip to accurate bridal diagnosis is recognizing your role in the situation. You are *not* here to change your bride or to alter her behavior. You are here to support her and her behavior—no matter how insane it may be! This is the theory behind "Supportive Therapy," a technique many real-life therapists use. Supportive therapists realize that even attempting to change their patients' behavior is a lost cause. In fact, pushing their patients to change how they behave would actually be destructive to their patients and to those closest to them.

The same thinking applies to your bride. Any dramatic shift in her behavior could make the situation worse for her—and more important—far worse for you.

So read on about each bridal personality and then circle which symptoms best suit your bride. If she presents some of the listed symptoms, you've found the right diagnosis.

The Granola Bride

Symptoms

- The wedding location is her favorite lake in Vermont.
- The dessert at the reception will be Ben & Jerry's Cherry Garcia.
- The plan is to adorn her hair with organic flowers.
- The shoes for the event? What shoes? She's going barefoot, of course.
- The bridesmaid dresses are from the Patagonia catalog.

Must-have therapies

The key to supporting this bride is remembering how much she loves all things natural. For a wedding gift, consider a donation to the National Wildlife Society or PETA. When complimenting her on the big day, forget words like "modern" and "chic." Try using words like "real, natural beauty" and "authentic love" instead.

The City-Obsessed Bride

Symptoms

+ Her wedding *must* be in New York City, Chicago, or L.A. No exceptions.
+ Her dream reception location is that swanky loft downtown with no name on the door.
+ Her transportation will not be a rental bus for the guests. Instead, she expects them to hail cabs.
+ Her dress will be Donna Karan New York. Who else?

Must-have therapies

The City-Obsessed Bride needs to be reminded constantly of how "in the know" she is. Throughout the wedding preparation process, be sure to tell her, "You know the best people!" or "This is truly a hot spot!" Also be certain to let her "school" you a bit on the latest and greatest trends and people. For example, when she tells you, "He is the hottest floral designer in town!" you simply tell her, "Really? You are such an expert."

But just because the City-Obsessed Bride is obsessed with, well, all things city-like, doesn't mean you have to get swept up in all her Sex and the Cityness.

Just because you can't afford the engagement gift from Barney's and just because you'd rather not spend your hard-earned money on Manolos to go with your bridesmaid dress, there's no need to fret. And there's certainly no need to reinvent yourself—or take out a loan—for your bride's sake.

The Indecisive Bride

Symptoms

- She *still* hasn't decided where the wedding will be. It's in five weeks.
- She took eight months to pick out her dress—and only made the decision once her mother forced her to do so.
- She took two weeks to decide to say yes when her fiancé proposed to her.

Must-have therapies

To help this bride make the decisions she's dreading, the secret is making suggestions in such a way that she believes the ideas are her own. Take Elly H., whose Indecisive Bride was so indecisive that she refused to pick out bridesmaid dresses for her five closest friends. Finally, Elly H. took it upon herself to go to the local bridal shop, pick out a dress, and bring it to her bride for approval. The next day, the bride told all the bridesmaids, "I have found the perfect dress!"

Way to go, Elly H.! The bride took your suggestion, but she made the idea her own.

The Control Freak Bride

Symptoms

- She controls all wedding planning. Seriously, her fiancé might not even know he's engaged.
- She's mandating that the bridesmaids wear their hair in a bun wrapped precisely the way Martha Stewart would approve.
- She requires her wedding planner to provide specific details of his precise location twenty-four hours a day.

Must-have therapies

The best way to cope with brides who feel the need to control everything is simple: give them control. When she asks you to be somewhere at a certain time, make sure you show up on time. When she asks you to tailor your dress to "floor length," make sure it perfectly grazes the ground.

Even though you may be cursing her under your breath, just do what she says for the next few months. In the end, the Control Freak Bride just wants a sense of calm and security. Be nice. Give it to her.

To understand the Control Freak Bride further, read on about Bridal Case File #19.

Bridal Case File #19: Lisa N.

Lisa N.'s bride could only be described in one word: Princess.

And what does every princess want? A fairy-tale wedding, of course!

Lisa N.'s bride had been dreaming of the magical wedding since she was four—maybe even three and a half. And when you had twenty-two years to plan a wedding, you can only imagine how perfect it just *had* to be.

The bride picked the place for the reception ten years ago: the Knightsbridge Castle in the mountains of Montana. She sketched her image of the perfect Cinderella-like dress on hundreds of pieces of paper throughout the years. She found the perfect horse-drawn carriage. The most eye catching tiaras. Yes, I said tiaras, plural. There were two of them— one for the ceremony and one for the reception. Even the most flawless Snow White-like makeup.

As her maid of honor (MOH), Lisa N. was a true champ. Using her Bridal Mode skills, she dealt perfectly with every piece of princessness thrown at her: hearing about the bleach-white horses, discussing the precise blend of rice to throw at the end of the wedding, and reviewing the ins and outs of their honeymoon plans at Disney's Magic Kingdom. Where else would a princess take her honeymoon?

But when the bride asked Lisa N. to carry a magic wand down the aisle, explaining that Lisa N. had been like "a fairy godmother to me," Lisa N. knew the bride's vision had gone too far.

"Are you crazy? People will laugh in my face!" she wanted to tell her. Instead, Lisa N. channeled Bridal Mode and told her, "Sure thing."

Bridal vision unharmed. Bridal crisis averted. Nice job respecting the vision of this control-obsessed princess to be, Lisa N.!

But just because the Control Freak Bride needs to control *everything* in her wedding, doesn't mean she needs to control *your* life. That's why it's critical for you to continue to do all the things that make you the sassy, savvy woman you are. Keep giving it your all at work. Keep taking things to the next level with your man. Keep attending those Spanish classes at the Y. Do whatever it takes to maintain a strong sense of bridal normalcy and control in your life—no matter how much pressure she puts on you.

The Low-Key Bride

Symptoms

+ She's chosen the chef for the reception to be Ronald. Ronald McDonald, that is.

+ She has a philosophy on finding the right dress, "When it hits me over the head, I'll take it."

+ When her fiancé asked her to marry him, she replied, "Sure, why not?"

Must-have therapies

Low-Key Brides are some of the easiest to support. She probably won't stress you out. She'll probably stay out of your hair. That said, it's important to remember that The Low-Key Bride—despite her nonchalant attitude—still cares about her wedding and wants you to care about it too. Be sure to ask her questions about the wedding preparations and about how she's feeling. And be certain to constantly ask if there is anything she wants to talk about or that you can do for her. Just because she seems not to care doesn't mean you can't show her that you do.

The Posh Bride

Symptoms

+ She's told you about the special treatment she received at the Oasis Day Spa like five times already. You get it. She's very well taken care of.
+ She has a hairdresser named Frederic Fekkai. No really, the real guy.
+ She's decided that just in case a head of state chooses to stop by the reception, all the guests are required to complete a background check.

Must-have therapies

When working with a Posh Bride, be sure to indulge her fancy side any chance you get. What's a great wedding or shower gift? A day at the city's finest spa. What's a great way to show her that you care? A shopping spree at Bloomingdales. Even if you can't afford the same bag she's buying, you can help her decide between the Marc Jacobs hobo and the Cole Haan clutch.

The Drunken Bride

Symptoms

- She's been drunk every day this week. Really, you counted.
- She has chosen favors? Bottle stoppers
- When you ask her about the proposal, she tells you, "I don't really remember."

Must-have therapies

The best way to support the Drunken Bride? Approach her carefully. Sit down to discuss her itsy-bitsy drinking issue. But proceed with caution. If she's resistant to change, now isn't the time to suggest she go to AA meetings or save herself from herself. That comes after the honeymoon.

The "My Mother Owns the Wedding" Bride

Symptoms

- The bride's mom calls you more often than the bride does for advice about the big day.
- The bride's philosophy on planning the event? "I'm just planning on showing up. My mom's taking care of it."
- The bride's not sure where the reception will be held because her mother has yet to decide.

Must-have therapies

This advice is tailored to support the bride's mom. Above all, remember: do not treat the bride's mother like your own mother even if she calls you nearly every day and has a knack for making you feel the same sense of guilt that you once thought only your *own* mother could. Make sure you continue to show respect for her mother and for the bride. Call her back when she calls you. Thank her for hosting you at every event. Be respectful at every cost.

The Anti-Bride

Symptoms

+ The invitation reads "jeans optional," *not* "black tie optional."
+ The ceremony will be at city hall. Or the city dump.
+ The chance of a manicure? You'll be lucky if she bothers to trim those babies herself!

Must-have therapies

The Anti-Bride just wants to *be* married, not *get* married. So she does not respond well to suggestions to "follow tradition" or "pamper herself." Remember that before you tell her, "Treat yourself to that expensive dress. You deserve it!"

Also remember that if you've landed an Anti-Bride, then you're in luck! Given her disregard for the fuss of matrimonial rituals, she'll likely put less pressure on you to adhere to traditional bridesmaid roles or take on annoying tasks.

The Rush-to-the-Altar Bride

Symptoms

+ She's pregnant.
+ She's afraid he's cheating on her.

- She doesn't care where they get married, just as long as it happens. This month.

Must-have therapies

Insecurity. That's what's plaguing every Rush-to-the-Altar Bride. Your job? Don't question her frantic behavior. Instead, do what any good friend should do and help her build up her self-confidence. Compliment her as often as possible. Remind her what a great friend she is and what a great fiancé she has. Do whatever it takes to make her feel as good about herself as possible. Once her confidence is restored, she may stop the rushing around.

The Runaway Bride

Symptoms

- Her type is the opposite of The Rush-to-the-Altar Bride, she still hasn't picked a date.
- Her feet are cold. Really, feel them.
- Her new favorite exercise machine at the gym is the treadmill. She runs every day without fail.

Must-have therapies

Like the-Rush-to-the-Altar Bride, insecurity is often the root of the problem for the Runaway Bride. She's scared to death of taking that walk down the aisle. To help, empower her to get to the heart of her insecurities. Is she insecure for valid reasons? Has her fiancé done anything suspicious? Has the BTB seen her parents experience something troubling in their marriage, such as divorce? If so, be there to talk her through these potential issues. Be there to calm her down as much as possible.

The Permanently Panic-Stricken Bride

Symptoms

+ She hasn't smiled in two months.
+ She answers her cell phone at all times, even when it's a telemarketer.
+ She has a contingency plan for everything.

Must-have therapies

Think about when things are crazy in your life, how do you relax? You get your nails done. You take a nap. You retreat to a quite corner at Starbucks.

You need to apply the same thinking to the Permanently Panic-Stricken Bride. Become her soothing tea, her relaxing massage, her quiet time. Become the one person who can calm her down in the insane bridal world that she's created for herself. Help her by offering to get your nails done together at a tranquil salon. Ask if there are any tasks you can take off her hands, like picking up Aunt Jesse at the airport or selecting the right favor for the shower.

Beyond supporting the Permanently Panic-Stricken Bride, you must create a limit to how much you can indulge her bridal panic attacks. Your limit is truly up to you. It could be the moment she calls you at 3:30 A.M. to remind you to bring your pink pumps to the dress fitting or the time she suddenly starts ranting about the number of tomatoes on the salad plate for the reception. No matter what it is—know your limit.

And once she reaches it, recognize it. It's absolutely acceptable to let her know that you need a bridal break, even if for a day. Or, perhaps a week. While your reaction may cause another panic attack in and of itself, your PBT guarantees that you'll feel better today and that she'll forgive you in the long run.

The Sublimely Calm Bride

Symptoms

- When you see her, she always looks like she just got back from vacation.
- When she discovered that the priest couldn't make it only two days before the wedding, she calmly sighed, "Oh, well. We'll find someone else."
- When the wedding date needed to be changed *after* the invitations had gone out, she decided to make her own invites. "No biggie" she said. "I like arts and crafts."

Must-have therapies

The key to supporting this kind of bride is realizing that the sublime calm on the exterior is actually a sign of the panic she's really feeling on the inside. So be careful *not* to pressure her too much. For example, when Stephanie L. once pushed her bride's buttons, innocently asking why she was so at ease about the fact that her wedding dress came in the wrong color, the bride completely lost it. In fact, she went from Sublimely Calm to Permanently Panic-Stricken. You don't want that to happen, now do you?

The I-Wish-I-Were-Still-in-College Bride

Symptoms

- Her choice for getting married is her college chapel.
- Her professor is the wedding singer.
- Her wedding favors are stuffed animals in the shape of jumbo elephants, her college mascot.

Must-have therapies

The I-Wish-I-Were-Still-in-College Bride is pretty harmless. And she may even be kind of fun to deal with, especially if you attended college with her. Her wedding experience may end up being a fun chance to reminisce — an opportunity to relive those fantastic four years. Just be sure not to hook up with the entire glee club this time around!

As a wedding gift, consider a donation in the couple's honor to the school's new library. At the wedding shower, consider making a scrapbook, complete with pictures and collections from your blissful bacheloreatte years together.

The Eco-Chic Bride

Symptoms

+ Her co-workers call her "the female Al Gore" when she's not around.
+ Her invitations were specially printed by a Native American tribe on organic paper.
+ Her food at the reception will not only be organic but also preservative-free, gluten-free, lactose-free, and flavor-free.
+ Her flight to New Mexico for the honeymoon will not happen. Instead, the couple is chartering a Toyota Hybrid.

Must-have therapies

The Eco-Chic Bride is all the rage right now. Similar to the Granola Bride, but a bit more politically minded, she's game for anything that sounds or looks green. Consider sending her reports on the latest bridal trend, Green Weddings, complete with recyclable cakes and organic flower decorations. As a gift? What else but a donation to her favorite green charity?

It's also important to note that the Eco-Chic Bride will become mighty eco-vigilant during the wedding prep process. Be sure not to let the water run too long when you're washing your hands in the ladies room with her. Make sure she doesn't catch you throwing your newspaper or soda cans in the garbage with the unrecyclables. If she does catch 'ya, prepare yourself for a super-green tirade!

The I'm-So-in-Love Bride

oms

ead is so far in the clouds, her skin is starting to
mulous.

time she hung out with you, your deep conversa-
nterrupted by your bride texting her fiancé
"OMG, I missed U soooo much in the past
"

to being asked if she's excited about the
ust can't wait to marry the love of my
vomit.

Must-

Tha   look of love! It's enough to make us
non-F   heads! The key to stayin' cool when
dealir   ove Bride is—embrace it! Go over
the   gifts like a framed picture of the
duo or   couples massage. Or how about
cooking   ppy two?
Don't   . Give in to the love.

The I-Could-Care-Less-About-My-Fiancé—It's-the-Wedding-I-Want Bride

Symptoms

- When her fiancé asked her to marry him, she took one look at the large ring and said, "Score!"
- She hasn't told her fiancé where the church is located. After all, he's not that important.
- She's been creating her "ideal wedding" scrapbook since she was five. She just left an empty space for a picture of the groom's head.

Must-have therapies

The thing to remember when dealing with this bridal personality is that her wedding is hands down, by far, the absolute most important thing in her life. Ever. More important than the groom to be.

No need to ask about her husband. No reason to question her about work. Think all wedding, all the time. When she calls, ask her how the planning is going. When you have coffee with her, discuss the intricacies of the reception. She may seem wedding obsessed. And she probably is. But the key to your successful survival? Just play along as long as you can. Well, at least until the wedding's over!

The Hippie-Chick Bride

Symptoms

- She hid a reefer in her bra to take a quick "hit" before walking down the aisle.
- She made a wedding list consisting of songs by the Grateful Dead, Bob Marley, and Dave Matthews.

♦ She refused to buy wedding shoes. Instead, she's planning to wear Birkenstocks under her dress.

Must-have therapies

Often confused with the Granola Bride and the Eco-Chic Bride, this flower-power princess is a breed all her own! Dig out your tie-dyed shirts and start playing some Jimi Hendrix. Get in the mood for a nod-to-the-60s time.

When selecting your gift, consider a collector's edition of her favorite artist or even a new bowl. Just because you gave up pot years ago doesn't mean she has!

But remember, when dealing with this Phish-obsessed female: just because she's laid back and free-spirited about the process doesn't mean you'll be free of responsibility. In fact, her marijuana-induced attitude may require that you take the reins a bit more than you are used to with other brides. For example, many Hippie-Chick Brides will leave dress shopping and location selection to the last minute. That means you may have to help her find the perfect organic cotton bridesmaid dresses or scout out the right outdoor spot for the tented ceremony. Be prepared to pick up where your Hippie-Chick Bride often leaves off.

The Jersey/Long Island Bride

Symptoms

♦ Her name is Gina. So is her hairdresser's.

♦ Her favorite show, the *Sopranos*, was filmed one town over from where she grew up.

♦ Her first dance will be to Bon Jovi's "Never Say Good-bye."

Must-have therapies

The key to managing the Jersey Bride is treating her like the City-Obsessed Bride. Every girl from Jersey or Long Island seeks the style, sophistication, and sass of women from the big city. So even if her Fendi is a fake and her hair looks nothing like Gwyneth Paltrow's, keep reminding her how chic and stylish she is in her own way.

Great gifts are special treats from New York City. Gift certificates from Barney's or Bergdorf's will give her a chance to put on her favorite "city outfit" and have a field day, thanks to you.

The Sexpot Bride

Symptoms

+ She's looking forward to the bachelorette party at Man Fantasy Land more than the wedding itself.
+ She tore a giant slit down the side of her wedding gown. On purpose.
+ She spent more money on lingerie for the honeymoon than she did on the wedding dress.

Must-have therapies

The Sexpot Bride is an unusual one. You *thought* that her endless hook ups in college and her not-so-occasional dancing on top of the bar at Coyote Ugly would end once she got that ring on her finger. But, alas, you were wrong. This chick just won't calm down. And the key to supporting her? Whatever you do, do *not* try to tame her. Leave that to her future husband. After all, he's seen her flash enough sailors during Fleet Week to know what he's getting himself into.

Trust me, you don't want to have happen to you what happened to Linda F.! When she tried to have a heart-to-heart with her wild-child BFF, it didn't go so well. She told her, "I'm sure your fiancé doesn't like the fact that you're still coming home at 2:00 A.M. without him and *with* twelve phone numbers." The bride's response? "You're completely taking his side!" In the end, the bride decided to drop Linda F. from the bridal party and the two stopped speaking for three months.

The-Money-Is-No-Object Bride

Symptoms

+ Her dad's name is Donald. Trump that is.
+ Her budget for wedding flowers is more than the down payment on your house.
+ Her wedding planner is the greatest. You know, the one who regularly works with Oprah.
+ Her dress is Vera Wang all the way. Meaning Vera Wang personally stitched it for her.
+ Her bridesmaids are Nicki and Paris. Hilton that is.

Must-have therapies

Maybe money is no object for this bride, but most often money *is* an object for you. So don't give in to the pressure to buy that $400 knife set from her registry. Try out a personalized scrapbook or photo album instead.

When she asks you to spend $300 on hair and makeup for your walk down the aisle as her bridesmaid, tell her you're doing your makeup and hair on your own. If you're not close enough to confess that you can't afford such royal treatment, just tell her, "I don't trust anyone but my Mario for my locks!" She'll understand.

The Unafraid to Be Cheesy Bride

Symptoms

+ The reception will be at Disney World. Mickey and all.
+ The wedding favors are framed pictures of the bride and groom with "So in love" written above their heads in puffy bubble letters.

Must-have therapies

The Unafraid to Be Cheesy Bride is very similar to the Jersey/Long Island Bride at first glance: same bigger-than-life hair, same desire for all things over the top.

But don't confuse the two. Unlike the Jersey/Long Island Bride who needs to be told how sophisticated and savvy she is, this bridal babe requires completely different treatment. She's actually pretty well aware of the fact that she's gone over the top.

What does that mean for you? Embrace the cheese! Help her create fun, insanely cheesy bachelorette party gifts like penis pasta and purple boas. Print out T-shirts for the bridal party that read, "I'm with the sexiest bride in the world!" Most likely, you'll only have the honor of working with one or two brides who are this self-aware of their high cheesiness factor. So have fun with it!

The "Got Tears?" Bride

Symptoms

+ Her skin is so thin, you can see through it. Really.
+ She's shed more tears than Kirstie Alley's shed pounds in the past few years.
+ She's so delicate that she makes flowers look tough.

Must-have therapies

Many BTBs demonstrate symptoms of the "Got Tears?" Bride at some point along their journey to becoming a bride. The difference between all of them and the *true* "Got Tears?" Bride is that the "Got Tears?" Bride stays sensitive *all* the time. So be ready with the Kleenex!

Jen L.'s bride is an excellent example of the "Got Tears?" Bride.

Bridal Case File #22: Jen L.

In the case of Jen L., her bride's wedding conjures up memories of just one thing: tears, lots and lots of tears.

Jen L. should have predicted it. She knew very well going into the process that her tear-prone co-worker was a true perfectionist. And when she demanded perfection but did not receive it, the result was a barrage of tears every time. Like the time the bride's dress came in two days later than planned. Tears. Or like the time the napkins turned out to be fully scalloped on the edges instead of lightly scalloped, the sound of sobbing could be heard two cubicles over. Each time, Jen L. was there to wipe away the tears.

And on the day of the wedding, when the hairstylist showed up thirty minutes late, the tears came rolling down.

When the hair maven finally arrived, he told the bride, "I can't wait to jazz up your hair!"

But the bride couldn't hold back. "Where have you been?" She scolded him as a tear burst from her just "done up" right eye. "We've been waiting here for thirty minutes!"

The bride continued to bawl him out as she balled herself into a tizzy. In the end, her makeup needed to be reapplied, the hairstylist discounted her $250, and her tears managed to be contained for the rest of the Kleenex-free evening.

Your PBT Says: You Still Love Her, No Matter What Her Personality

Let's face it. No matter what the diagnosis, she still means the world to you. That's the thing about brides. As impossible and flustered, self-centered, and out of touch with reality as your BTB can get, she matters so much. Or at least she used to. And she will again—once her wedding is over.

So when she goes on one of her rants about making sure your hair is perfectly teased or brags about the "killer" service she's getting from the city's best salon, cut her some slack. Remember:

- She won't be a bride forever.
- She still has some goodness hidden underneath those layers of eyelet somewhere.
- You, too, may have a diagnosable bridal personality one day.

CHAPTER THREE

Stage III: Masquerading

*Playing the part of good friend during every
inning of the unending wedding game*

Your PBT Says: When She Goes Crazy . . .
So Do You

I held my bride's hair back for four hours while she puked in
the grimiest dive bar in DC the night before the wedding.
—Anonymous, Baltimore

I held her Swarovski crystal-adorned dress in the air while
she tried on what seemed like 10,000 different types of cream-
colored shoes: Closed toe. Open toe. Slingbacks. Platforms.
They just *had* to go perfectly with the gown. It was too
much—even for a gay man like myself.—Peter P., Chicago

I drove all the way from Santa Fe to San Francisco *just* to
give a two-minute toast at her engagement party. I then turned
right around and drove back to start work at my new job
the next morning.   —Jessica F., Santa Fe

At my bride's request, I sang "You Are So Beautiful" while she
walked down the aisle. I was so nervous that I nearly fainted
before I uttered the first verse.   —Aliza L., Indianapolis

My bride issued a "no kid" rule at *her* wedding. When the best-behaved five-year-old in the world showed up that day because his babysitter had a family emergency, my bride whispered in my ear, "What is *that* doing here? Get rid of it!" I had to find a polite way to escort the young mother and child out of the church." —Megan H., Ft. Lauderdale

When you ask women, "What is the most insane thing you've done for your bride?" they are invariably eager to respond. As if they've been waiting for someone to ask them, so they can get it off their chests. Most will tell you, they've done it all. They've glued down bangs, held clammy hands, hand-stamped envelopes and hugged that lonely groomsman, all in the name of the bride.

And I'm sure you have a lot of horror stories yourself. Right? Like the time you took three days off from work to help her find the *perfect* strapless gown or the time you cancelled your family vacation to be back in time to attend her bridal shower or the time your boyfriend threatened to "call it quits" because he was so sick of renting tuxes for all your friends' weddings.

If you've never thought about it before, take a moment to reflect on the most insane thing you've ever done for a bride. Jot down your craziest story in the space provided. If you need extra room to vent, feel free to write a few pages in your journal. It will feel good to get it out—just remember to keep it well hidden. You don't want your bride, or anyone else for that matter, getting ahold of such incriminating evidence.

Go, ahead, this space is for you:

_____

_____

_____

_____

_____

Your PBT Says: Thank You!

Yikes! Those are some ghastly bridal tales—you have truly gone above and beyond. And if your bride hasn't said those magic two words for going those extra bridal miles, then I will: "Thank you!" And if she hasn't told you recently, take it from me, you're a great friend.

"If I'm so great, why do I need to read this chapter?" you wonder. Good question, my bridal precious.

This chapter isn't *just* about being a good friend. More importantly, it's about you being good to yourself along the way. It's about teaching you not only how to *survive* the bride but also how to *thrive* throughout Stage III: Masquerading.

Your PBT Says: Practice Makes Perfect When It Comes to Stage III

Masquerading—or playing the part of good friend—is the next secret weapon in your wedding arsenal, guaranteed to help you wade through even the treacherous waters of Stage III. Give it a try:

1. Close your eyes.

2. Picture your least favorite food in the entire world. It may be simple, like Aunt Hanna's chopped liver. It may be sophisticated, like raw eel at Nobu. All that matters is that you imagine the one food that makes your stomach turn.

3. Imagine putting that undelectable delight into your mouth.

4. Wait, before you go making a horrible face or turning to gag, imagine that your biggest crush in the world is sitting across from you. Maybe it's Brad Pitt. Maybe it's Brad Garrett.

Maybe not. There's really no accounting for taste in this exercise.

5. What would you do in a situation like this? Of course, you wouldn't dare show an ounce of disgust. You can't complain, make faces, or spit out the nastiness in the back of your throat. The only thing you *can* do is — smile.

This way is exactly how successful masquerading should feel, no matter how bad a taste your bride's behavior leaves in your mouth or no matter how badly you want to bop her in the head with a crystal tiara or barf on her white shoes. It's time to be — or at least pretend to be — the great friend you know you are.

So grab your "Best Friends Forever" half-heart necklace. Dig up those pics of your variety show duet at Candy Mountain Day Camp in third grade. Do whatever you need to do to remind yourself of why you were friends to begin with, and get cracking at being her friend — no matter what.

To start, let's take a bridal test-drive of how to cope with Stage III with a few hypothetical situations. Get your driving mocs ready!:

Your Pearly Whites vs. Her Wedding Wish

It's late. Monday night. You just got root canal and your mouth is severely swollen. Seriously, you look like a chipmunk on steroids. The doorbell rings. Your bride enters and asks you to be her MOH. Your response?

a. "Um, okay. It's hard for me to be happy right now with this . . . *cough* . . . cotton lodged in my throat."

b. "You know I'm not really into that kinda stuff. But, why not?"

c. "I can't wait! This is a dream come true to be in your wedding. Maybe the swelling will have gone down enough so that I look decent for your wedding pictures."

The correct answer: c. Why? This answer shows over-the-top enthusiasm and a bit of self-deprecation to boot.

Your Must-Have Lovin' vs. Her Bridal Needs

You're enjoying a romantic evening alone with your hotter-than-usual boy toy — the first time in months that you're actually able to pucker up without your roommate lurking in the next room. Just as you're about to make a tipsy toast to your "special time together," the phone rings. You know from the "Here comes the bride" ringtone that it's none other than your bridal BFF. Your response?

a. Don't answer it. You're about to get some much-needed lovin'.

b. Don't answer it now, but send her a text message telling her that you're thinking of her and that you'll call her first thing in the morning.

c. Answer it just to make sure she's ok, listen to her stories for a few minutes, and then ask if you can call her back first thing in the morning.

The correct answer: b or c. Either answer is acceptable in this instance. You need to be there for her, but you also need to prioritize your time to get hot and heavy with Mr. Handsome.

Your Weekend Wants vs. Her Dress Distress

It's a beautiful Saturday morning in the city. You wish you could spend it outside enjoying the first nonrainy weekend in weeks, but you are forced to try on what seems like every bridesmaid dress ever made. Seriously, every single one.

After having gone to eight stores and having tried on 8,000 dresses, your bride asks if you would mind going to one more store that's "not *too* far away." Your response?

    a. "Absolutely, boss! But after this one, I've got to get home."

    b. "I'm getting really tired. Can we just pick from the dresses we've seen so far?"

    c. "I can't. I've got to get home to catch up on my TiVoed soaps. I'm so behind."

The correct answer: a. Again, as much as it kills you, you've got to go along with her on her bridal journey. But be certain to let her know that you've got a life of your own to live.

Your Eight Hours of Zs vs. Her Wedding Nightmare

The phone abruptly wakes you out of your Taye Diggs–starring Hawaiian vacation dream. You barely read the clock—it looks like 2:30 A.M.—and you remember that you have to give a huge presentation at 9:15 A.M.

You answer it and, of course, it is your bride. She's fully frantic about the fight she just had with her fiancé. Apparently, they just couldn't agree on the seating charts; should her college friends sit with his friends or sit separately? Your response:

    a. "Well, let me think about it. Hmm, I think it would be really nice for everyone to get to know each other and sit at the same table."

    b. "I'm too tired to think about tables."

    c. "Sweetie, at the end of the day, it doesn't really matter where people sit. Everyone will be dancing and having so much fun, they won't even care."

The correct answer: a or c. Of course, a is the preferred answer — it is polite and thoughtful; c is a creative way to at least calm her down.

Your Stage III Score

If you answered at least two of those questions correctly, you're well on your way to masquerading mastery.

If you got just one — or even none — of the questions right, don't worry your pretty little head, my dear! Masquerading is a skill that requires just what the doctor orders — no, not an apple a day — but real-life practice with real-life brides.

Just think that the more brides you have in your life, the more practice you'll get. I'm sure you just can't wait!

Your PBT Says: Learn What to Expect When She's Expecting to Get Married

Now that you've sharpened your masquerading skills, this section will teach you how to apply your skills to real-life occasions along your beyond bad bridal journey — from endless engagement party to honeymoon horror. If you're a bridal novice, this'll be especially helpful for you.

What to Expect at the Engagement Party

The engagement party can range from a no-fuss night out at the local bar in cutoffs to a swanky soirée that rivals most wedding receptions. The key to successful masquerading at the engagement party is to remember: tonight is *all* about celebrating the most exciting two minutes of your bride's life—when she said yes to her fiancé, what she was wearing that night, what the ring looked like, how he "popped the question," how she felt, how he cried, how long it took her actually to answer him. Tonight is *all* about *all* the excruciating details.

The key to surviving the unending engagement party minutia? Masquerade, baby!

Bridal Case File #1: Kathy B.

When Kathy B.'s best friend from college announced her engagement, Kathy B. knew life would never be the same. Her bride was already a big talker—one of those friends who likes to provide every possible detail of every moment, from the cost of her morning coffee to the length of her evening commute. Kathy B. knew that adding wedding planning to the bride's life would add even more delectable details to her daily stories.

When it came time for the engagement party, Kathy B. and her hubby drove four hours to her bride's family estate in Massachusetts. When the bride's mother opened the door, Kathy B. instantly understood where her bride got her knack for detail-oriented chatter. This Mother of the Bride (MOB) would just not stop!

"Kathy! It is so great finally to meet you! When I woke up this morning, it was about 6:30. I thought to myself, 'It will be so nice to meet my daughter's friends from college.' You know, when I sent out your invitation—it was on October 9th—I sent it in the morning to make sure that it went out from the post office as early as possible. Did you receive it the next day?"

Apparently, this MOB expected Kathy B. to have the same knack for non-important details. Rather than tell this detail-obsessed woman, "I have no idea—I don't keep track of those things!" Kathy B. simply smiled. She knew what she had to do—be the best friend she could—even when dealing with this wacky woman.

"You know what? I did get it the next day. It must have been October 10th." Kathy B. purposely played right into her game.

The rest of the not-so-engaging engagement party was filled with more toe-curling details than anyone would ever care to remember. From the Mocha shade of Origins lip color the bride was wearing when he proposed to her to the year of the "half Cab, half Merlot" wine they drank to celebrate to the strapless La Perla bra the bride wore with her strapless sundress "that kept bunching up."

But Kathy B. kept her cool. With her masterful masquerading skills in her back pocket, she knew what she needed to do. She remembered that her job was to smile, nod, and say only positive things about the magical engagement.

By the time the event ended, Kathy B. knew more about the bride, the groom, and June 27th—the day they became engaged—than anyone should ever know.

What to Expect During the Dress Selection Process

It takes some pretty powerful masquerading skills to cope with the dress selection phase. So many seemingly unimportant questions will cloud your bride's head.

Does she want cream? Off-white? Diamond white?

Does she want strapless? Spaghetti straps? Sweetheart neck?

How about lace? Satin? Tulle? Chiffon?

What about couture? Or the dreaded off-the-rack?

Inevitably, the questions will trickle down to you, whether or not you care to answer them.

To maximize masquerading during the wedding dress selection, the key is to be honest, but not too honest, when doling out dress advice. Remember, your bride only wants to hear good things. So when she asks for your attire opinion, be certain to sew in at least one compliment. Take it from Sarah F., a fellow survivor of a dress-obsessed bride: compliment the bride every chance you get!

Bridal Case File #36: Sarah F.

When Sarah F. was called in to help her close co-worker find the perfect gown, the situation was already in a "code-orange" state of wedding emergency. Her bride had over-analyzed, intellectualized, and agonized over her dress choice for the past six months. Seriously, her bride had spent every weekend visiting nearly every bridal store in all the Midwest. No dress had gone ungroped or untried on.

Sarah F.'s bride desperately needed an impartial decision maker to step in and help her before it was too late to order the dress in time for the summer wedding. Finally, her bride narrowed the decision down: either (1) a strapless number with intricate beading down the sides from Macy's or (2) an overly ornate marshmallow fluff ball from Marie's Specialty Store or (3) a somewhat see-through sheath, which showed every dimple on the bride's booty, from Bloomingdales.

Of course, the smartest choice was the elegant gown from Macy's. But rather than overtly scream out her opinion, Sarah F. remembered that she was dealing with an irrational bride. She took a deep breath and gushed to her bride, "The

strapless dress from Macy's is the kind of dress only someone with your body could wear. It would be punishing the
dress if you didn't wear it. You look breathtaking."

Well, that did the trick. Sarah's bride went with the most
tasteful, and shall we say most flattering, number.

Sarah F.'s lesson? In her own wise words, "Compliment
her to close the deal."

What to Expect at the Bridal Shower

In case you didn't have enough wedding events to attend or
come up with an excuse *not* to attend, the wedding gods just *had*
to tack on the bridal shower. Time—yet again—to shower the bride
with love, affection, and attention. As if she didn't already have
enough!

The bridal shower usually takes place at a restaurant or a relative's home, often on a weekend. It's typically a luncheon that
takes place about a month or so before the wedding day. If you're
in the wedding party or a close friend of the bride, chances are
you'll be planning or helping to plan this bash. Lucky you!

Remember, no one, especially not you, wants to attend yet another ooh-and-ah-filled ten-hour-long event at the pancake house
three hours away. So remember the "big C": Creativity!

I know what you're saying: "I sure don't have a creative bone
in my body!"

The last time you were asked to be creative, your fifth-grade
teacher held up your *To Kill a Mockingbird* book report in front
of the entire class as an example of what *not* to do.

Well, put all those creative memories aside, my patient! This
time 'round, there's no pass or fail at school. Being creative is
much easier in this case.

All you have to do is ask yourself, "What does my bride like to do?" Is she a swimmer? A dancer? A writer? Once you've come up with your answer, you've got your bridal shower theme, and you've got yourself in her graces for the rest of the wedding process.

Here are a few creative—and truly personalized—bridal shower ideas that may spark some new thoughts for you:

♦ For the girly girl: Spend a special "spa day" indoors, complete with professional manis, pedis, and massages, right at home from local spa employees. And the perfect gift for the BTB: ask each attendee to purchase a funky nail polish color and write a quick story about why "Tropical Nights" or "Naughty Red" reminds her of the bride.

♦ For the dancer: Nothing beats private dance lessons at the local dance studio for the bride and her friends. Perhaps invite some of the groomsmen to the last hour for a special performance.

♦ For the workout fanatic: Go private trainer all the way! What male trainer wouldn't love anything more than to get a bunch of bridal cuties into shape for the afternoon?

♦ For the outdoorsy type: Create an outdoor-only day of hiking, followed by horseback riding, and bbqing. As a shower gift, ask each guest to bring a story of the bride to share over s'mores.

♦ For the movie buff: Nothing beats a girls-only night at home. Rent three of her favorite flicks, grab a bowl of gourmet popcorn, and order the guests to wear their pj's. Gift bags for the attendees could include classic wedding DVDs such as *The Wedding Planner* and *My Best Friend's Wedding*.

♦ For the cultured: She wants culture? Give it to her. Pack your day with a trip to the latest exhibit at the MoMA, followed by the latest off, off, off Broadway show.

♦ For the cook: Gourmet cooking lessons with the gals and the local French pastry expert is a great way to bond — and practice your French. Bon Appetit, anyone?

For more inspiration, check out Stephanie S.'s story.

Bridal Case File #20: Stephanie S.

When Stephanie S.'s best friend since college asked her to be a bridesmaid, she was thrilled! Unlike many of us who dread wearing those unfabulous, frilly frocks and standing behind the bride *yet again*, Stephanie S. was honored to perform every not-always-so-fun-for-the-rest-of-us bridesmaid duty.

One of her duties was the planning of the bridal shower. Stephanie knew she had her work cut out for her; her bride was the opposite of a girly-girl, so no day at the spa or tea party would do.

She started brainstorming for ideas by writing a list of her bride's hobbies: bike riding, hiking, painting. Then she thought about taking the guests out for a bike ride or a hike along Lake Michigan, but she knew that the guests in their fifties might not be up for it. Just when Stephani S. was about to resort to a boring luncheon at the local bistro, it hit her — like a drop of paint, literally. While she was walking home from work in her Chicago suburb, she felt a drop of something icky on her shoulder. Alas, it was a child shaking off his paintbrush enthusiastically.

"What is this artistic munchkin doing?" she wondered. Her eyes went up above the four-footer and she read the sign on the store window, "Pottery Painting for All Ages." She knew she had found the perfect spot for the bridal shower!

She negotiated with the owner and booked a Saturday night in June for a night of pottery painting and drinks.

In the end, the guests painted the town—well, at least some pottery—red. The event was a shower success, all thanks to Stephanie S.'s creativity.

The other key to surviving the bridal shower is remembering that no matter how involved or uninvolved you are in planning the shower, the bride's mother, or MOB, often deserves all the credit. While it's typical for the bridesmaids to plan and pay for the shower, these days the MOB is the planner and financial backer of the bash. And you don't want to forget it.

If you find yourself in the oh-so-typical situation in which the MOB is running the bridal shower show, your role is simple: volunteer to help the boss of the bash at every turn. As soon as the engagement news strikes, call the MOB to ask if you can help prepare for the bridal shower. As the bridal shower date approaches, send the MOB an e-mail or give her a call to see what else you can do. And on the day of the bridal shower event, get there early to help Mom however you can.

Bridal Case File #16: Lori R.

When Lori R.'s little sister announced her engagement, Lori R. *knew* that their mother would take the reins. Nicknamed "the host with the most," their mother had waited twenty-six years to host this "wedding to top all events." And when it came to the bridal shower, even though Lori R.—the MOH—technically *should* have been the one in charge, their mother would simply not stand for it.

To start, Lori R. handmade the cutest invites. But their mother proclaimed, "They are nice, but really should be printed on high-end stationery. That is the right thing to do." Then Lori R. selected a casual bistro on the lake as the ideal spot for the party. But their mother strongly recommended the town's more sophisticated country-club setting instead.

Rather than go with her gut and fight her all the way, Lori R. realized that she was never going to win this battle. It was their mother's vision, and there was no point messing with it.

In the end, the shower was a tasteful success. And when the bride thanked Lori R. for "a wonderful time!" Lori R. responded, "Thank mom. It was all her," and winked at her mother.

What to Expect at the Bachelorette Party

Be prepared, my bridal beauties, for the debauchery, the cheese, the silliness that *is* the bachelorette party.

Whether the night involves furry handcuffs and strippers in Vegas or pink slippers and female bonding at home, the important rule to remember is, the bride wants to be the center of attention, even when she says she doesn't. She's dying to wear the homemade crown, to kiss the boys at the dive bar, to do some very silly things, even when she says she's not.

Remember, this may be your chance *not* to listen to the bride for once. Score!

When she tells you, "I don't want anything wild and crazy," that's code for "Bring it on, baby!"

When she says, "Please don't make me wear anything silly," she's really saying, "I can't wait to try on my 'Tonight's my last night as a single lady, boys' T-shirt."

And when she urges you, "Please don't make me do anything

embarrassing," she's really trying to tell you, "I can't wait until you make me say 'hi' to random men at the local pub."

Your job? Make her the center of attention at all costs. Embarrass her till the cows come home!

Read on about the perfect example of how Briana G. tackled this task.

Bridal Case File #49: Briana G.

Briana G.'s bride was the oh-so-typical woman who "did not want a big fuss" for her bachelorette party." What a liar!

She told Briana G., "Please don't make a big deal out of it."

So when Briana G. set out to plan the event, she took her bride's advice way too much to heart and tried not to go over the top. That's where she made a big mistake. You always want to go over the top.

Her plan? A simple backyard BBQ, complete with bandanas and beer. Briana G. thought that the slightly over cooked burgers and footlongs were a great success. It turned out that the bride thought otherwise

While ending the evening with Coronas and lime, the bride told Briana G., with tears running down her cheeks, "I wish you and the other bridesmaids had done more for this day!"

Briana G. immediately removed her "Kiss The Cook" apron and sprang into Bridal Mode. "I'm so sorry," she told her bride. "When you said not to make a big deal out of this day, I really thought you meant it."

In the end, Briana G. did all she could to make the event special, ordering a limo on the fly and taking the girls out to the local hot spot to continue the celebration—ketchup and mustard stains and all!

Lesson learned. Masquerading required.

What to Expect at the Rehearsal Dinner

Just when you thought you'd heard every single story about the couple. Just when you thought you'd been told every nice thing about the bride and groom. There's always room for more at the rehearsal dinner!

In fact, the rehearsal should feel like you pressed "repeat" on an engagement party song that continues to play over and over again.

These days the rehearsal dinner has evolved far beyond an informal gathering for the bridal party. Today it is a night of toasts, fanfare, and celebration of the wonderful bride and groom.

To masquerade your way through this one, prepare your ears to hear more about two people than you ever thought humanly possible. Get your arm in shape to raise your glass to toast them more times than you can imagine!

To survive, remember that the night will have to end eventually. Keep your cool, just like Maya K. did.

Bridal Case File #31: Maya K.

This is the tale of 10,000 toasts.

Maya K. was best described as a "veteran bridesmaid." She'd been down the aisle in bridesmaid dresses in nearly every color of the rainbow; she'd mastered the techniques of bustling the bride's gown, throwing the perfect bachelorette party, and finding just the right thing to say at rehearsal dinners. In fact, other bridesmaids came to her when they needed tips on crafting the right toast or speech.

You want something funny? Maya K. knew how to make even the most uptight wedding crowd crack up. You want something sentimental? Maya K. could have 'em in tears in no time.

When it was time to prepare a toast to her bride at what

Maya K. swore was the tenth rehearsal dinner she'd been to that year, Maya K. didn't bat an eyelash. She prepared a simple, yet thoughtful, toast for the evening. She printed out her kind words on embossed stationery and gently wrapped her toast in a satin bow.

Sure, she may have borrowed a few lines from other toasts she'd given in the past, but Maya K. was certain the bride would love it. She proudly carried it with her to the event at the San Francisco Cultural Museum Hall. Little did Maya K. know who her competition would be.

The night got off to a fun start. Drinks were flowing. Food was being devoured. And then came the toasts. Maya K. figured that the groom's fraternity brothers from Penn State would make some fumbling, drunken speeches. That's where she was oh-so wrong.

The first fraternity brother opened his speech with a song—complete with guitar backup—that he wrote for the bride and groom. It was eerily touching.

The next normally brazen brother presented the couple with a basket that was full of gifts he collected from around the world; each gift represented a special trait of the couple. It was actually really sweet.

But when the next guy pulled down the shades, opened his computer and began to project a professional PowerPoint presentation, complete with Photoshopped images of the bride and groom, Maya K. realized that her dinky poem was doomed.

Who would have thought that these drunken dudes would get their act together? PowerPoint? Presents? Songs?

"What is going on?" she wondered.

Just when she thought that the competition couldn't get any fiercer, the last fraternity king took the stage.

"I know how much you two like to drink," he began.

"Thank goodness!" Maya K. thought. "He's just going to make some sophomoric alcohol joke," she told herself.

"So," the frat boy continued. "I traveled to Napa where I worked with a team of wine specialists to create your very own customized wine. Here's the first bottle with your name inscribed in the glass." When the crowd cheered with delight, Maya K. knew she'd officially been outdone.

When it was her turn to make her toast, she felt defeated inside but kept her head up and made it through the toast. It may not have had PowerPoint animation, nor did it involve cultivating grapes in California, but it was short and sweet. And the bride loved it. The lesson learned for Maya K.: always go with your gut.

Despite Maya K.'s temporary wavering of self-confidence, she stuck with her story and gave those frat boys a real, heartfelt run for their money.

What to Expect on the Big (Wedding) Day

From taking overly posed pictures for what seems like hours to making friends with complete strangers at your table to dancing with way-too-eager men twice your age—or sometimes half your age, brace yourself. It's time to put your masquerading skills into full effect!

The wedding day is the culmination of all her fuss, all her muss, and all her craziness that has driven *you* crazy. But just because the insanity will soon come to an end, doesn't mean the wedding day itself will be a complete honeymoon. On the contrary, you need to be ready to deal with the bride in her zaniest state, to cope with relatives who just *"have* to meet you," and to deal with any unforeseen disasters that inevitably occur on the big day.

Take Josie Y.'s wedding day disaster and read on.

Bridal Case File #8: Josie Y.

Before Josie Y.'s bride got engaged, she was the picture of poise. If something went wrong at work or at home, she'd been known simply to say with a perfect smile, "No biggie," and go about her happy life.

The moment that ring slid onto her finger, however, poise left the building. In walked emotional instability.

Throughout the wedding planning process, Josie Y.'s bride was an emotional wreck who let anything and everything get to her. The day of the wedding was no exception. For Josie Y., that meant she had to work very hard to help her bride fight off tears and anxiety the entire day.

To help her bride stay calm, Josie Y. suggested that the bride have half a glass of champagne. The bubbly seemed to have a positive impact. That is until the bride decided to get behind the wheel. As the bride drove herself to church, her emotions somehow got the best of her driving skills.

The next thing you know, police sirens were ablaze and the bride was pulled over. Already in tears, she started to tell the officer, "Today is my wedding day. I'm sorry that I swerved a bit."

"A bit? You were all over the place!" he told her.

Luckily, Josie Y. had been driving right behind her bride and saw the entire dreadful event unfold. She immediately sprung from her car—in her emerald bridesmaid gown and Nine West silver pumps—and marched right over to the state trooper.

"Sir, this is my best friend. It is my fault that she had half a glass of champagne today. I thought it might calm her down. If anyone is going to be punished, it should be me."

The seemingly unflappable officer was apparently so taken by Josie Y.'s selfless act that he let the bride go with just

a warning. And in the end, Josie Y.'s actions made sure that
her bride made it to her own wedding!

What to Expect at the Post-Honeymoon Hangout

You'd think that the moment you send your bride off on her
Hawaiian honeymoon, you'd say a happy farewell to masquerading. Unfortunately in most cases, that's not the way it goes. You'll
need to keep the smiles coming and the "I'm so happy for you!"
statements flowing for some time. At least until the first time you
hang out with the bride after the honeymoon.

Just when you think you can let your bridal guard down, be-
ware. There will be pictures. There will be stories. There will be
details about honeymoon sex and U.T.I.S—usually more information than you want to know. But perhaps the most shocking
part of the post-honeymoon hangout is how different your now
married bride may be.

In many cases, you'll find that she's gone from being one of
your most stylish, self-motivated friends to playing the part of
the "good wife." Here are a few telltale signs to expect:

- She's proudly sporting the "I'm married now" bob—hav-
  ing cut off several inches of her once-long locks.
- She utters the "When we have a baby . . ." statement.
- She's changed the screen on her cell phone now to read
  "Wifie" instead of "Alexandra."
- She has to cut your coffee date short to rush home to
  cook *him* dinner.
- She's begun talking about how she needs to stop dyeing her
  hair. After all, you can't dye your hair when you're pregnant.

- She's wearing an "I'm married now" loose-fitting sweater instead of her normally tight tank.

So, what's a girl like you to do when the woman formally known as your BFF suddenly seems unrecognizable? You've got it— masquerade. In fact, this is likely the last time you'll need to dig up your masquerading skills. So, be sure to make the most of 'em. That means:

- "Ooh and ah" when she whips out picture #321 from her photo album.
- Squeal with forced delight when she revisits the too much bridal information (TMBI) details of her wedding night.
- Count your bridal blessing that this is finally the last time—at least for now—that you'll need to use your masquerading skills.

Your PBT Says: Help Your Friendship Thrive Throughout the Process

What's the last trip to take on your masquerading journey? While the number-one priority in any bridal situation is you, of course, your number-two priority is maintaining your friendship with your bride.

It's one thing to *pretend* to be a great friend, as you learned about throughout Stage III, but it's another—and more important—thing to remain true friends. To do so, learn about the six unspoken rules of staying friends with your bride. Even when you're ready to say "uncle."

1. *Remember your own feelings:* No matter how wrapped up in her "bridal world" you become, the key to staying friends is remembering yourself. Recognize your own feelings. Ac-

knowledge when you're feeling sad or jealous or happy or bitter. After all, just because she's the one getting married doesn't mean that you're any less important in this relationship.

If things get sticky between you, tread with caution but be certain to let her know how you're feeling. Remember, she may be a bride, but at her core she still wants you as her friend.

2. *Be there (for her) or be square:* It doesn't matter how jealous you are of her or how big of a pain in the Bally's-sculpted butt she is. Be there. Fly the distance to the shower in Detroit. Go the extra mile with that extravagant gift. In the end, you'll feel better about yourself knowing that you were there for her.

3. *Do it with a smile:* It's true. No matter how miserable you are or how badly you want to tear that ring off her finger, if you're smiling, you'll feel better. Seriously—just try to be mad or even shed a tear while you're showing off your pearly whites. It's impossible. A smile is guaranteed to make you happy—if not, at least it'll make this whole experience a bit more bearable.

4. *Good things come to those who wait:* Remember, her state of bridal insanity is only temporary. A year from now, the last thing on your mind will be how angry you were because you just spent your entire weekend trying on horrid bridesmaid shoes. Your friendship with her is more important than the wedding frustrations. Just wait it out, my friend.

5. *Think glass half full:* Even if your nickname is Ms. Negativity, you need to stay positive during the masquerading phase.

Here's a helpful trick: Pick your favorite memory of your friend. Maybe it's that time you went canoeing freshman year in Maine. Perhaps it's that blistery trip you two took to Denver to follow those cute ski instructors. Whatever memory it is, keep it at the top of your mind. Whenever she's driving you crazy, close your eyes, count to ten, and then imagine that moment. It'll keep you thinking positive.

6. *Respect the ring:* From now on, every time you see your bride, you must ask to see the ring. This is your way of continuing to acknowledge that you've accepted her engagement and that you're happy for her—even if you're secretly not.

And, hey, if it's a nice sparkler, try it on for yourself.

Your PBT Says: You Win!

Well played, you masquerading mama, you! No matter what the score, you've made your way through Stage III victoriously! I hope so has your friendship with your bride, and more importantly, I hope so has your own sanity.

As you continue to play the wedding game throughout the next stages of this bridal duel, feel free to return to this chapter. Use it as a refresher for what to expect at each phase and to reignite your masquerading skills whenever you need a boost.

CHAPTER FOUR

Stage IV: Anger

Dealing with bridal jealousy, loss,
and self-doubt

Your PBT Says: Check *Almost* Everything Off Your Grown-Up Wish List

Pottery Barn–decorated apartment. Check!

Calvin Klein shades you always wished you could afford. Check!

High-paying, high-powered job of your dreams. Half a check!

Adorable VW Passat. Check!

Balenciaga hobo bag. Double Check! (Anything that expensive deserves two checks.)

Overall sense of happiness. Check!

There's no shame in admitting it: you're living the sweet life. And don't you deserve it? You've spent your entire life gearing up to be a real-life "grown-up."

And here you are—grown up. Yup. You're happy. You're successful. Look at you, all cute and mature.

So what's with the long face? Why is your stomach tied in

knots? What's with that twinge of nervousness you feel when someone asks, "What's next for you?"

I know the answer! I know! Call on me, your PBT!

It's all that pent-up anxiety, that hidden jealousy, and, yes, that ripe anger. It all stems from the fact that you've reached that difficult stage of life in which everyone around you is getting married. The stage of life in which you spend every weekend as a bridesmaid and every weekday sulking at home.

Yes, this is the stage in which you woke up one morning and realized that, *kazaam*, everyone you know is suddenly "happier than they've ever been in their lives"—either seriously dating, currently engaged, or already married. Every one of your friends is busy planning that special day, enjoying their honeymoon, or sending out "thank-you" cards proudly featuring the new last names they've just taken.

"Excuse me?" you ask. "When did all this happen? How did I miss the secret dole out of 'happily-ever-after' pills?"

The answer, my bridal babe, ain't so pretty. The truth is, this stage of life sometimes stinks. There ain't no sugarcoating it.

And to make matters worse, no one really prepares us for this time in our twenties and thirties. Without warning, it seems that you've got more married friends than single friends—when it used to be the other way around. Or you're the only one who wouldn't describe your relationship as "perfect," as the rest of your friends would.

Face it. No immaculately decorated bachelorette pad, no exciting career path, not even a shopping spree at Fred Segal's— well, erase that one—can magically undo the uneasy feelings inside you. Only dealing with them head-on will do.

But have no fear—your PBT is here. And, trust me, no one's sat through more weddings, heard more engagement announcements, or dealt with more sullen nights home alone than this bridal expert. And lucky for you, this way-too-experienced PBT has devoted this entire chapter to helping you drudge up and deal with your "struggle behind the seams."

To see if you're ready to take on Stage IV, take this quick "Are You Bitter?" quiz. Put a check next to any of the symptoms that sound familiar.

- ☐ You've been to more weddings than first dates in the past year.

- ☐ Your wedding-obsessed friends' vocabulary has suddenly changed from "getting wasted" to "getting measured" and from "Chinatown karaoke" to "fine china."

- ☐ You've been a bridesmaid so many times that the saleswoman at Kleinfeld's Bridal not only knows you by first name but asks if you'd like to join her for lunch. Again.

- ☐ You've "winked" at everyone on match.com under the age of forty-five and even chatted with a guy named Glen who *claims* he's just turned eighteen.

- ☐ You've taken your mom up on "going on just one date" with Gary Bornstein, whose winning credentials include owning a Long Island car dealership.

Did you put a check next to two or more of the symptoms in the quiz? If so, you've got a bit of bitterness in that cute little bod of yours. But that's to be expected when it comes to the Anger Stage.

Welcome, my dear, to the most challenging stage in Bridal Therapy, Stage IV: Anger.

Your PBT Says: The First Step in Dealing with Anger Is Actually Finding It

If you ask most therapists—even those not as immersed in the bridal world as your PBT—about anger, they will tell you something quite surprising. Anger does not always surface outwardly in the forms we are used to seeing it, such as yelling, fighting, or arguing. In fact, for women more than for men, anger is oftentimes expressed in very passive, even self-destructive ways: gossiping, avoiding eye contact, making do with second best, setting yourself up for failure, overeating or under-eating, and avoiding conflict.

Sound familiar? I thought so.

"What? Me, an angry person?" you ask. "No way!"

Even if you don't consider yourself an angry person, this stage of life has probably made you angry or insecure on some level. And it's time to face that anger head-on—or veil on, if you will. Take the "Anger GPS Test: Find My Anger" that follows to locate precisely the hidden anger lurking somewhere deep inside your highly successful self.

"Anger GPS Test: Find My Anger" Directions

1. Read each of the questions that follow.

2. Without giving it too much thought, circle either *Y* or *N* to each question.

3. Count the number of *Y*s.

"Anger GPS Test: Find My Anger" Questions

In the past six months, have you . . . ?

1. Given someone the silent treatment. Y N

2. Gossiped about a close friend. Y N

3. Spoken badly about someone behind her back. Y N

4. Pretended to cry. Y N

5. Played sick. Y N

6. Avoided conflict in some way. Y N

7. Overeaten or under-eaten for longer than ten days. Y N

8. Overslept for long time periods. Y N

If you answered yes to two or more questions, there's definitely some anger going on there. I knew it! In order to determine where that mysterious anger came from, look back at your Yes questions. Think about the situations that provoked those responses.

Did any of them have to do with your current relationship or, umm, lack thereof? Were any of your reactions triggered by an unconscious fear that all your friends will soon leave you to be married? Did your bride's announcement of her honeymoon in Rio leave you wondering, will *my* honeymoon be as grand? Did your mother's nudging last week about when *you'll* be the one sending out invitations get to you more than you thought?

Give yourself a few minutes to reflect on these situations. Use this empty space to write down at least three places from where your anger may have stemmed:

1. _____

_____

2. _____

_____

3. _____

_____

Your PBT Says: Take Time Out for Anger Management

Congrats—you've successfully located that dreaded anger. You've gotten past the hard part of Stage IV. Unfortunately, this psychological wizard can't entirely erase your anger with a magic wand. But she can certainly help you manage it.

According to the American Psychological Association (APA), it actually wouldn't be a very good idea if we could eliminate anger entirely. Life—especially during this stage—is inevitably filled with situations that cause anger. You can't change that. But you can change your reaction. Your very own PBT has borrowed the APA's top anger-management tips and rejiggered them especially for you. Read on.

Bridal Anger-Management Technique 1: Chillax!

You could have guessed it yourself, right? One great way to ease some feelings of anger is to relax.

Here's a great way to relax called the "Empty Chair" technique. Give it a whirl:

1. Find a somewhat private place.
2. Close your eyes.
3. Imagine your favorite beach in the entire world. Maybe it's Malibu. Maybe it's the Greek Islands. It just has to be *your* favorite.
4. Feel the sand between your toes. Hear the water crashing on the shore.
5. Picture, now that you're nice and comfy, that there's one empty beach chair next to you.
6. Fill it with whomever you'd like. Your current boyfriend.

The man of your dreams. Your husband. Whomever you'd like to share the perfect beach with.

7. Gaze into his eyes. Hold his hand. Take a deep breath.

8. Count to three, open your eyes.

9. Ask yourself, "Don't I feel relaxed?" Your answer should be a resounding, "Yes!"

Another great way to relax is with the help of one, shall we say, accidental therapist—Maria Von Trapp from *The Sound of Music*. Don't tell me you don't absolutely love this queen of positive thinking!

Whether it was escaping the convent or the Nazis, this girl overcame it all. And thanks to her, you can use her technique, aptly named "A Few of My Favorite Things" to quell your anger.

1. Start by popping in your DVD of *The Sound of Music*. If you don't have it on DVD, you should be ashamed of yourself. In that case, simply download it from iTunes or rent it from Netflix.

2. Find the storm scene in which the Von Trapp kids—all twenty-nine of 'em—pile into Maria's bedroom for a much-needed pep talk.

3. Sing along with Maria about all of your favorite things, whether that means raindrops on roses or sales at Barneys.

4. Play it at least twice, and you're guaranteed to feel calmer— and much happier—than you did five minutes ago.

Bridal Anger-Management Technique 2: Master the Art of Cognitive Restructuring

Let's call on the psychology gods yet again for help with your anger-management issues. This time, it's Ellis and Beck, famous cognitive therapists in their day, who'll help us. Perhaps they didn't treat women coping with the horrors of modern-day brides, but that won't stop your PBT from borrowing their technique: Cognitive Restructuring.

Let's get down to business, shall we? Cognitive Restructuring is just a fancy phrase coined by these therapists to make themselves feel more important. It's really a pretty simple concept. The word "cognition" means thought, and the word "restructure" means to rebuild. Hence, Cognitive Restructuring means to re-structure—or change—the way you think.

In this case, it means to replace your angry, irrational thoughts, such as "I am going to kill my bratty bride!" with more rational, achievable thoughts like "My bride is really frustrating me right now, and I need to spend some time away from her."

Let's practice some Cognitive Restructuring. Write down five statements about your bride or about your feelings toward this stage of life. Feel free to be a bit overly dramatic just for effect.

1. I feel . . . _____
2. I feel . . . _____
3. I feel . . . _____
4. I feel . . . _____
5. I feel . . . _____

Now go back to each of these statements, and using Cognitive Restructuring, restructure each sentence in a more positive, more actionable way. Ellis and Beck recommend that you cut out words like "always" and "never." They'll just make the problems seem worse, as if there were no way to solve them.

Restructure 1. _____
Restructure 2. _____

Restructure 3. _____

Restructure 4. _____

Restructure 5. _____

As you continue along your bridal path, try to practice Cognitive Restructuring as much as possible. You'll start to feel less angry—and more hopeful—in no time. Thanks, Ellis and Beck!

Bridal Anger-Management Technique 3: Send in the Clowns!

A good chuckle never hurt. Except the time your dentist laughed out loud at the X-ray he took of your teeth and yelled, "This one's got a horse's mouth!"

Seriously, according to the APA, humor is a recommended way to diffuse anger. These experts suggest a good chuckle now and then. Their reco? What I'm calling the "Picture It" technique. Here's how it works:

1. Try this the next time you get angry enough to call someone a name, such as Bride from Hell. Stop and picture what she would actually look like with that imaginary name.

2. Picture her with devil horns, fiery hair, and flames instead of Jimmy Choo's on her feet. You may even want to draw a picture of this Devil Bride.

3. Do this whenever a name comes into your head about your bride or about anyone else causing you anger. And you'll be laughing in no time.

According to anger-management specialist Dr. Deffenbacher, another way to deal with anger is what your PBT is calling the "I Am a Goddess" technique. Dr. D. created the technique based on what he's learned about angry people. Angry people tend to believe that "things oughta go my way" all the time. When they don't, angry people get, well, angry.

Try out his "I Am a Goddess" technique. It's actually pretty fun:

+ Picture yourself as a goddess, a supreme ruler, if you will. You rule the world, shop anywhere you want—even Barney's and Neiman's. No matter where you go or what you do, everyone bows down to you and does exactly as you command.

+ Imagine the streets paved with gold, the bars serving only your favorite drink, your boss telling you to take more time off, and Saks never out of your size 8.5 shoes.

+ Get real. After a while, you'll probably start to realize that being ruler of your universe is a bit crazy. It's unreasonable to think that everything will always go your way.

+ Apply this technique to the next rumble with your bride. When she asks you to stay a few minutes later than planned to help her pick out the perfect pantyhose, re-member what you learned as queen of the world. Things may not always go as you perfectly planned. And that's okay.

Bridal Anger-Management Technique 4: Change Your Scenery

Paris. Rome. Monaco. What do all these places have in com-mon? I mean, besides the hot men with fabulous accents? You guessed it! They're all places other than where you are right now. Whether you're reading on the train or in bed in your cramped apartment, these places beat yours by a landslide. And sometimes, they're all you need: a change of scenery.

Of course, you don't have to jet to France or boat to the Bahamas—although that would be nice. Sometimes your immediate surroundings are what cause anxiety and anger. Try out these tips to escape:

+ Schedule "personal time" without your bride, without any weddings to prepare for, without getting ready for your next blind date.
+ Take a walk around the block to your favorite park or to your favorite shoe store.
+ Go ahead and "regretfully decline" the next wedding function. Everyone needs a real break once in a while.
+ Work it out and walk her off. It's true, getting physical at the gym is a great spot to forget all about your bride.

Once you take on anger, it's time to move on to her evil twin sister: jealousy.

Your PBT Says: Admit It—You're Jealous As Hell

Admit it, no matter how hard you force a smile, no matter how tight you hug your Bridezilla, no matter how genuinely happy you are for her, there is a bit of jealousy—an offshoot of anger—buried deep inside you.

Do you feel a pinch in your stomach when she shows off the ring to passersby?

Do you wince when she describes her over-the-top place settings for the reception?

Do you shudder when she tries on her hand-sewn Monique Lhuillier?

If you answered yes or even maybe to one or more of these questions, it's official! You're jealous, baby.

For some of us, jealousy is far worse than for others. For unmarried chicks, jealousy often hits particularly hard: all the attention, all the love, all the hoopla. It is enough to make us non-ring-wearing women of the world want to puke.

When will it be *your* turn? When will *you* have the chance to impress your friends with fancy cutlery? When will *you* get to plan a special day when *you* are the center of attention, *you* call all the shots, and *you* parade around in a tutu-like gown? When is that day when *you* will have the authority to make your friends wear dresses in your favorite color, even if it is taupe?

For married matrons, feelings of jealousy may be a bit more tempered. You've been down the road—or the aisle—firsthand. You know that what seems like wedding bliss is often more like a nightmare. But that doesn't mean you don't look at your bride and wonder, "Why did *she* get to do it right?"

How did *she* book that band that never called you back? How did *she* manage to afford that tailor who sewed her gown perfectly against her slim frame? Who did *she* hire for those perfectly golden brown, honey highlights—the ones that look exactly like Jessica Alba's, not the Melanie Griffith-like highlights you got?

Then there are those of us who refuse to admit that we're jealous. We live perfect lives. We feel perfectly happy. "Why would her joyous occasion make me jealous?" you wonder. Well, it's time to face up to the facts, sister—you're jealous too. Read on for the top ten signs that you're secretly jealous of your bride:

The Top Ten Signs You're Secretly Jealous of Your Bride

10. You're planning to wear white to her wedding reception. Why should *she* be the center of attention?

9. You felt a fleet of butterflies swarm your stomach when

your BTB called to share the big news. You figured it was indigestion.

8. You caught yourself imagining how her dress would look with *your* coloring.

7. You once found yourself comparing the salaries, the waist sizes, and the number of chest hairs of your own boyfriend/ husband with her fiancé.

6. You watch when her fiancé reaches over the dinner table to kiss her hand at dinner, and you think to yourself, "Why isn't my man as romantic as hers?"

5. You've tried on her ring more often than she actually wears it.

4. You notice your boyfriend/husband is balding. So is her fiancé. Why does it look sexy on hers and geeky on yours?

3. You can see your entire reflection in her ring 'cause it's so gosh darn big.

2. You still haven't returned the message she left on your voice mail announcing her engagement. It's been two months.

1. You're busy planning the fourth weekly "Singles Only" night out for the girls. Your bride isn't invited.

If any of these signs sound even vaguely familiar to you, you're probably jealous.

But, you're probably more familiar with jealousy—the emotion Shakespeare called the "Green-Eyed Monster"—when it comes to your love life, not your bride's life. Like that time you caught your normally one-woman-kinda man checking out that blond chickie at the supermarket. Or the time you ran into his ex on the street, and she looked more like a *9.5* vs. the *6* he told you she was.

Jealousy can occur in any relationship, however. And just like anger, jealousy is a powerful mixture of emotions. Unlike anger, it's less about frustration and feeling slighted. Jealousy often stems from a real—or imagined—loss of someone. In this case, it's the loss of your bride.

That's right. Oftentimes an inevitable sense of loss comes along for the ride when your bride is getting married. You may wonder:

"Why is she leaving me for him?"

"Who will I watch *Saturday Night Live* with now?"

"Will *he* be her new emergency contact?"

To cope with your bridal jealousy, there are three steps you must tackle.

Step 1: Admit it.

The first step to overcoming jealousy is to admit there's a problem. So, go ahead, admit it:

+ Now repeat after me, "I'm jealous."
+ Now try saying it out loud.
+ Now write it down on a piece of paper or type it into a word document.
+ Now that you've admitted the problem, I know you're ready to change. Good girl!

Step 2: Get to the root of it.

> *To cure jealousy is to see it for what it is,*
> *a dissatisfaction with self.*
> —Joan Didion, author

Joanie was right! The not-so-fun part about coping with jealousy is realizing that it sometimes comes from your *own* feelings of insecurity. So ask yourself the questions that may be causing your jealousy. For example:

♦ "Is her fiancé more important than I am?"
♦ "Am I hot enough to land my own husband one day?"
♦ "Will she drop me from our 'I love being single!' life for him?"

See how easy it is to let your own feelings of self-doubt get in the way?

Step 3: Boost your ego.

"Thanks, captain obvious!" you're saying to yourself. "I could have figured out this self-doubt stuff on my own!"

Perhaps. But you probably couldn't have figured out how to improve your self-esteem on your own. And that, my bridal beauty, is the key not only to overcoming jealousy but also to being happier in general. Next are a few ways to boost your ego with ease:

♦ Spend time with people who *always* make you feel great about yourself. Can you say, "Hi, Mom!"?
♦ Achieve something. It doesn't have to be a master's degree from Cornell in eighteenth-century Russian literature. But small successes, like creating a fab-o PowerPoint presentation at work or organizing a volunteer event on a random Saturday, will surely inflate your ego.
♦ Spend time doing what you love—whether that means jazzercising at the gym or singing your heart out at karaoke in Chinatown.
♦ Plan a date with your BFF from childhood. The one who knows how fantastic you are—and loves reminding you of it.

♦ Practice an act of kindness toward someone *other* than the bride. Buy coffee for your co-worker or give Grandpa a call to wish him "Happy Saturday." Putting a smile on someone else will surely make your own pearly whites pop.

Your PBT Says: Beware the "Ring Effect"

In addition to being wary of anger and jealousy — as if those were not enough — there's another ugly monster you need to keep tabs on during Stage IV.

It's a strange phenomenon sweeping the country. Suddenly, women's careers mean nothing. Their hard-earned MBAs are forgotten. When you ask them about women's lib, they say, "What's that?"

Today what matters most is no longer who you are and where you are headed. It is the size of your sparkly diamond ring. And women are going out of their way to ensure that their ring is the biggest, boldest, sparkliest one in town.

This is the "Ring Effect."

And we're not just talking about celebrities here. Of course, Katie Holmes' rock is the size of your hometown football field. Yes, Beyoncé's $5 million gem is bigger than the average toaster. But non-celebrities are heavily influenced by this trend, too, demanding bigger and bigger rings than they have before. Read on to understand the Ring Effect.

Bridal Case Example #38: **Mel S.**

If anyone knows brides, it is Mel S.! A part-time wedding photographer in New York City, Melissa S. has seen 'em at their best and worst. Plus, she has the pictures to prove it!

"I've noticed over the past few years that the size of rings has increased dramatically," she says. "They used to be big.

Then, they became huge. Today they are out of hand. Sometimes, it seems like the bride's ring is bigger than her wrist!" she reveals.

Mel S. met her photography nightmare two years ago. From the first meeting with this BTB, Mel S. knew the ring would be front and center. When introducing herself to Mel S. the bride told her, "It is nice to meet you. Would you like to pet the ring?"

When the bride put her hand out in front of Mel S., she literally gasped. Not only was the center diamond itself humongous, but the blue diamonds flanking it "put the Titanic necklace to shame!"

When the big day finally arrived, Melissa S. went about the usual business of snapping shots of the happy couple, the wedding party, and the reception area. With each shot, the bride made certain the ring was fully visible. She even convinced Melissa S. to spend an entire roll of film solely on the ring. In fact, the final album featured four pages specifically of the ring—closeups, black and whites, action shots, and stills.

Melissa S. left the event wondering what was more important: the ring or the marriage itself?

Okay, so rings are big. But what *do* you care about a chunk of sparkle? Well, your PBT has learned that the Ring Effect has an impact not only on brides, but also on women just like you—those of us living in the shadows of brides.

The Ring Effect makes us forget that it was just last week when she called you crying about how much her fiancé "sucks" or that it was just last month when her fiancé kissed another girl in Vegas. In essence, the Ring Effect sweeps away all your bride's issues and convinces you that your life could also become perfect, if only you, too, had a monster wedding sparkler.

When we see women wearing these insane gems, a funny thing

happens: Gone are any realistic notions of what the bride's life must be like. It is as if once she wears a ring, she has found the perfect man and is living the perfect life. Read on and take it from "The Salad Girl."

Bridal Case Example #45: "The Salad Girl"

Standing in line for her "super salad" at the latest salad hotspot in sweltering San Diego, "The Salad Girl" was destined to spend more on her salad than she did on her Miss Sixty jeans. As she debated in her head the nutritional value vs. the taste factor of chickpeas, a diamond sparkle up ahead caught her eye.

It came from the woman in front of her. She was the most perfectly petite woman—hair effortlessly swept up in a bun, Chloe shades gently placed on top of her head, super-cute sundress fit to a T. And to top it all off was a huge emerald cut of perfection.

But it wasn't the ring alone that got to "The Salad Girl." It was everything that came along with it. The ring stood for stability, for adoration, for a husband who cares enough to spend a fortune. It stood for a husband who would provide for her if she chose not to work, who would take her on trips to Europe, and who would spoil her with flowers at least once a week.

Somehow, the Ring Effect brought out all of this patient's innermost hopes, dreams, and insecurities.

Your PBT Says: Big Bling Does Not = Big Happiness

The question for you—yes, I'm sure you've guessed it by now—is, have you ever transferred your feelings over to a ring, like our friend "The Salad Girl"?

Ever spotted a glittery diamond and thought, "Isn't she lucky that she has a fiancé with such great taste?"

Ever walked by a jewelry store and thought to yourself, "Once I get one of these suckers, my life will be set?"

If so, remember, just because she's got the ring, doesn't mean her life is as grand as it seems. No jewelry in the world can replace happiness. You know that. Don't let her Harry Winston convince you otherwise!

Learn from the case example that follows.

Bridal Case Example #30: **Mona C.**

To understand Mona C.'s bride, one must first understand what kind of lifestyle this bride was living. Having grown up as the only daughter in a wealthy family in the suburbs of San Francisco, she could have any Mercedes, could attend any Ivy, and could tote any Coach bag she wanted.

And her "I've got it all" luck did not stop with material possessions. This bride was beautiful and smart. So she could snag any hottie she went after and land any job she wanted.

When it came time to select a suitor to spend the rest of her lush life with, Mona C.'s bride could have married pretty much anyone she wanted. Even a pauper with no money would have worked out just fine, given all of this woman's trust funds waiting in the bank

Of course, Mona C.'s bride did as the rich do and found a husband with just as much money, just as gorgeous a face, and just as well educated a brain.

But let's get back to the ring.

In Mona C.' words, "The ring was perfection." Mona C. had never seen anything like it before in her life. It sparkled with brilliance, it shined with charm, it framed the bride's hand with elegance. Complete strangers would stop this bride on the street just for a glimpse of this beauty.

So when Mona C.'s bride called her one late Sunday afternoon to explain that she'd canceled the wedding, Mona C. was in shock. Apparently, the bride's fiancé not only had a love for money, appearances, and education but also had a deep love for other women. Mona C.'s bride caught him whispering sweet somethings over the phone to another woman.

In the end, Mona C. learned that lots and lots of carats does not mean lots and lots of love.

Your PBT Says: Be Ringless and Proud

As you've learned, the Ring Effect hits many of us very hard. But in the case of many a bride, such as Mona C., the perfect ring does not mean the perfect life. In fact, having that finger free for a while is oftentimes the best way to go. To internalize this lesson, try this "Ringless and Proud" therapy:

1. Go to your bedroom or bathroom—anywhere private with a mirror. Stand up straight and look at your reflection. Repeat this phrase out loud: "My name is (complete with your name). And I am not wearing a ring."

2. Take your ringless identity for a spin. Once you've perfected the phrase in the privacy of your own home, try it out everywhere you can. Introduce yourself at parties as "Happily Ringless." Tell your co-workers to stop calling you Sergeant and call you "Ring Free" instead. Even ask your boyfriend to swap his "Pooh Bear" nickname for "Ringless."

3. Notice that your signature says it all. So start signing your e-mails and greeting cards as "Ringless and Proud."

Your PBT Says: Bridal Anger, Be Gone!

Congratulations—you've made it through Stage IV. As a symbol of your ring-free, anger-ridden self, complete this proven ritual:

1. Pull out that old pair of leg warmers from under your bed. Rainbow-striped ones are preferred.

2. Play "She's a Maniac" from *Flashdance* on your iPod. If you don't already have it, download it now.

3. "Channel" Jennifer Beals. Run up and down in place for ten seconds or until you feel energized.

4. Take out your pocket mirror.

5. Look directly at that hottie staring back at you. Say these words out loud: "Bridal anger, be gone!"

6. Really say it out loud this time.

Remember, no matter what comes your way over the next several months, you can handle it without anger and with calm and confidence.

CHAPTER FIVE

Stage V: Transference

*Reap the benefits of the bride
without all the fuss!*

Your PBT Says: Beat Your Bride at Her Own Game

Maybe it's the diamond ring. Maybe it's the personal trainer. Perhaps it's the lace gown that Olga from Russia hand made herself. Or the hoards of people doing as the bride commands at all times. Or the constant attention of friends and family. Or the pampering. The primping.

Maybe it's all these things rolled into one simple three-word phrase, "I'm getting married!"

These days, no other statement packs as much stopping power punch as a bride proclaiming that she's getting hitched. Simply uttering those words—the words she's been dying to say since she was eight—means so much—like the royal treatment at hair salons or countless sample dinners or "the works" at suddenly overly accommodating spas. Even somewhat inappropriate flirtation with gay wedding planners means something.

As if knowing that your fiancé loves you, having your future perfectly mapped out for you, and having an excuse to take three weeks off from work were not enough, today's brides are reaping some seriously extra-special fringe benefits when preparing to tie the knot.

But what today's BTBs do not realize is that they no longer get to keep their private perks to themselves. Thanks to your PBT's undying devotion to us non-brides of the world, I'm ready to unveil the must-know secret to coping with any bride—beating her at her own game.

That's right. It doesn't matter if your ring finger is barren, or if you are nowhere closer to marriage now than you were at the Junior Prom.

It is time to bring the best of the bride's life directly to you!

Stage V reveals the once-secret and once-reserved-only-for-brides techniques necessary to achieve "unwedded" bliss. That, my bridal friend, will make the transference stage without a doubt one of the most enjoyable stages of your Bridal Therapy. In fact, these techniques are the ultimate way to turn the feelings of jealousy and anger you learned about in Stage IV into excitement and un*bridled* pleasure!

Your PBT Says: Trans . . . Wha?

The last time you used any word beginning with "transfer," you were probably talking about transferring money from your *emergency-only* savings account back into your checking account to fund those adorable Tory Burch flats. Stage V, however, involves a different kind of transferring called "transference."

Our friendly friend, Freud, coined the term back in the early 1900s as a phenomenon characterized by the transferring of feelings that you have for one person to another person.

Here's an example that might help you grasp Freud's idea: Let's imagine that your fifth-grade teacher, Mrs. Messina, was this horrible Shrek-like creature who constantly picked on you, especially when you didn't know the answer in class. You just *hated* her.

Today your new boss walks into your office for the first time, bearing a striking resemblance to the grade-school ogre about whom you still have nightmares, funky breath and all.

Before your new boss even opens her mouth to greet you, you may have *transferred* some of your anger originally directed toward Mrs. Messina to your new boss. So no matter how nice your new boss may be, you unconsciously worry that she'll pick on you, just like monstrous Mrs. Messina did.

"So what in the world does this psychobabble transference stuff have to do with me?" you ask. Good question!

We're actually going to use transference in a new way, in a way Freud may not have intended. You see, when the pipe-smoking papa first came up with the idea, it was a pretty negative thing. And from the Mrs. Messina example, you can see why.

But leave it to your PBT to make things all warm and fuzzy! Your PBT is going to flip transference on its head and turn it into a *positive*.

In this stage, you'll learn to transfer all the benefits of being a bride—without all the anxiety and preparation—to yourself. This, my friend, is called Bridal Transference. And while Freud would probably roll over in his grave if he got wind of how your PBT has reshaped his original idea, Bridal Transference will have you rolling over with joy in no time!

Your PBT Says: Ask the Question You've Been Dying to Ask

Before we delve into the technicalities of transference, we need to explore the question on many non-brides' minds, "Do brides *really* have more fun?" According to the lovely ladies in the following case examples, the answer is a big, fat *yes*!

Bridal Case File #24: Janet Y.

Prepare yourself for the stinging dismay you may feel when you learn of the tale of Janet Y.'s bride. It is guaranteed to have you agreeing with your PBT in no time—brides do have more fun. Or at least more free bling.

Janet Y.'s bride was spared nothing growing up in her posh Miami pad. Cars, couture clothes, spur-of-the-moment vacations. You get the picture: Paris Hilton minus the sex tape.

When it came time for the wedding, she was the epitome of the "I Don't Care About My Husband, I Only Care About My Wedding" Bride. She'd been working with designers since she was eighteen to create the perfect gown, and selecting getaway honeymoon locations with her mother since she was twenty. And now that the big date was set, nothing but the bridal best would do.

Janet Y. had grown up watching her friend in awe since she was a child. So she was prepared to feel a bit jealous when the wedding preparations came 'round. But it wasn't the designer dress or the private beach reception that got to Janet Y.—she expected all that. Rather, it was the unexpected celebrity-like freebies and discounts her bride received.

The dress designer took $4000 off the price just because it was his "favorite customer's" big day. Her trainer took her in for free for three months. And the nail in the wedding coffin? The jeweler lent her a $35,000 necklace for the event.

This bride took full advantage of her "I'm getting married" status. Even though she could have afforded all these worldly pleasures and much more, she batted her BTB lashes every chance she could. Regular manicures were upgraded to "spa manicures" complete with massage. Hair appointments were moved up hours earlier to accommodate this bride's busy schedule. Even restaurants scheduled private dining tastings, clearing out many a table just for this princess.

Janet Y. spent the majority of the nine months of wedding planning with her jaw on the floor, continually shocked by her bride's behavior—and by the behavior of those cast under the "I'm getting married" spell.

But that didn't stop Janet Y. from taking full advantage of some of the benefits of her bridal BFF. Lucky for her, whenever her bride just *had* to get a manicure, Janet Y. joined her for moral support—and a polish change. Whenever her bride just *needed* to go for a much-needed drink, Janet Y. joined to help her bride deal with the stress of wedding planning—and to sip some bubbly for herself.

What lesson did Janet Y. so astutely learn?

When her bride turned to her at their hot stone massage appointments and said, "I could never do this without you!" Janet Y. responded, "Lucky for *both* of us, you don't have to!"

Way to take on transference, Janet Y.!

Your PBT Says: Get with the Transference Program!

Now that you know it for sure—brides, and sometimes their best friends, really do have more fun—there's no shame in admitting it. Come on, you know it's true.

We've all fantasized about becoming a bride, of walking down that perfect aisle and of kissing that supercute tuxedo-clad man.

But we're also smart enough to shriek at the thought of all the stress of planning a wedding. Now, thanks to Bridal Therapy, you can reap the benefits of the bride without the nightmare of finding Mr. Right, spending a fortune on the bank-breaking event, or getting engaged. That's what transference is all about — receiving the pluses of being the bride while skipping all the minuses.

Welcome, and thank you for enrolling in the exclusive "Benefits of the Bride" Transference Program! Just like any good exercise or therapy program, the key to this benefits package is truly committing. But once you learn about how incredibly fabulous this program is, you'll probably be more committed to this than you were to your post-New Year's diet. Besides, who can drink carb-free shakes for two weeks anyhow?

Be sure to take notes on the ultimate five-step program detailed ahead:

1. *Set the date:* Start by picking a day that will be exclusively for you and for no one else. Then clear the date with your boss.

   Once you've chosen your date, start getting excited about it. Mark the days with hearts on your planner; set the alarm on your BlackBerry. You may even want to hold an official "countdown" to the big day. After all, why should brides be the only ones with a special day to look forward to?

2. *Dress the part:* Begin by buying a really expensive looking pair of Nicole Riche-like sunglasses. This will automatically make you feel glamorous.

   Raid your closet — or Zac Posen's. Find your favorite outfit — the one that makes you look slim no matter what. Now is certainly not the time to experiment with those skintight jeans you *just* squeezed into or that halter from college. Trust me, trying on anything that you don't have a prayer of fitting into will do double damage to your fragile ego.

If nothing suits your fancy in your own digs, go for the Gucci gear at the store of your dreams. After all, if your bride gets to shop beyond her means for her wedding dress and other "bridey" outfits, you're entitled to do the same! Just be sure to be a bit practical. If you're going to splurge on a new sheath dress or satin scarf, ask yourself, "Will I really wear this more than once?" If the answer is yes, slap down the plastic. After all—unlike the bride who only gets to wear her gown one night—you have the luxury of wearing your new threads as many times as your non-married heart desires.

3. *Get your non-bride bootie in shape:* Why should brides be the only ones with an excuse to work on their perfectly sculpted arms? You, too, deserve to look like a million buckaroos.

   Start by hiring a personal trainer. Preferably, his name is Sven and he is from Sweden. Meet with your trainer on the morning of your special day—that way you can keep your tush tight throughout the rest of your day—and keep up the exercise, even after this program has ended.

4. *Spas—here you come:* Step four is all about doing what brides do best—pamper themselves beyond reason. Now it's your turn!

   Make an appointment at a super spa and order "the works." We're talking mani, pedi, facial, and massage.

   While you're there, you should also try out a Brazilian bikini wax. Sure the pain of the thirty-minute session may be hard to forget, but you'll feel oh so sexy for the next month. When you pay, *don't* look at the bill. Just throw down the plastic as any good bride would do.

Next, get your hair done. Nothing drastic—no color change or Japanese straightening unless you're really dying for an over-the-top transformation. A simple trim and blow-dry will be enough to put a smile on your deserving face.

5. *Toast the happy you:* Congratulations! You're finally, well—um—unmarried!

Sure, you may not be able to call yourself "wife." True, you may not be able to *legally* start using that new last name. But you sure can celebrate!

So send out the evites or, better yet, pick up some fancy invites from Kate's Paperie, and bring your besties over to celebrate the happy—*you*!

Go ahead and decorate your home with whatever color *you* prefer, even if that means hot pink. Select the appetizers that *you* like, even if that means the quintessential pigs in a blanket. Then, pop open some bubbly—and be sure to purchase the finest bottle you can find.

If a soiree is not your style, plan a more intimate dinner with a couple of your friends. Make a reservation somewhere you'd never even think of going—or think of affording. Let the conversation and the food flow. It's your time to revel in *you*.

Your PBT Says: Say So Long to Your Inner Bride for Now

By the end of Stage V, you will look great and you will feel great. But you will be ready to exit the "Land of Bridal Make Believe" and return to reality. Thank goodness!

I hope that, by playing the part of BTB, you now have a

deeper understanding of the benefits — and even the downsides — of being a bride. This knowledge will help you throughout the remaining stages of Bridal Therapy, whether or not you're accompanying your bride for dual manis and pedis or brushing the hair away from her face when she cries over her "destroyed" table settings.

More importantly, your PBT hopes that this Transference Program has transformed you into a happier, more energized woman — with or without the ring. And that you will depart from this stage with a strong sense of relief that you've got time for Sven to get your biceps into shape for your big day!

CHAPTER SIX

Stage VI: Fixation

Stop obsessing over her *wedding*

When she had a crush on Christopher Benito in fifth grade, so did you. When she asked for Posh Spice's haircut, but got Ashton Kutcher's, so did you. When she cried over those rainbow braces she *thought* would look awesome, so did you.

Today, as she obsesses over her wedding . . .

So do you.

But you don't have to. In fact, you shouldn't. There's a big difference between *helping* her plan for the big day and obsessing over it right along with her.

That's what Stage VI: Fixation is all about—recognizing and overcoming your obsession with your bride's wedding.

Your PBT Says: Face the Frilly Facts of Fixation!

"Wait just a minute there, missy!" you say. "I'm not the one obsessed with the wedding—my bride is!"

That's the tricky thing about Fixation. You may not *think* you're obsessed with her wedding, but in most cases—it's time to face the frilly facts. If you're reading this book, you're probably way more involved in someone else's bridal life than you ever thought you would be.

But before we can accurately gauge your level of inappropriate involvement in your bride's life, you must learn more about a wonderful word our good old friend Freud coined: "fixation."

Fixation is a psychological state in which you are obsessed with another person, object, event or ideology. It typically occurs when an issue from the past remains unresolved, leaving you focused—unhealthily—on something.

Same idea applies to your bride. When you are fixated on her wedding day, there is usually something from the past causing you to spend way too much time, energy, and emotion on her. Ask yourself:

- "Do I know why *her* wedding day is so important to *me?*"
- "Is there some aspect of our relationship from the past that I am still thinking about?"
- "Has she always gotten more than me? Have I always gotten more than her?"
- "Do I feel guilty over some event in our past? Am I trying to overcompensate now?"
- "Was I not there for her in some stage of her life when I should have been? Was she not there for me when she should have been?"

Take a few minutes to consider these questions and your answers, and feel free to revisit them as you journey throughout Stage VI.

Another reason so many of us tend to engross ourselves in our brides' lives is that we just don't feel so fabulous about our *own* lives. Sad, but oh so true. Take Jackie R.'s situation.

Bridal Case File #34: Jackie R.

Jackie R., age 32, had overused Bridal Mode so much that she forgot about the importance of her *own* mode—herself.

As the day to her big sister's wedding grew nearer, every moment of Jackie's R.'s life seemed to revolve around her sister. During the work day, she coordinated with the florist, confirmed orders with the caterer, and scheduled time for the bride to get a relaxing massage.

The wedding coordination did not stop at the end of the day. At home, Jackie R. spent far more time chatting with her sister on the phone about the intricacies of Vodka luges than she did taking care of her beloved dog or live-in boyfriend.

And any free time Jackie R. had left was spent getting into shape for the big day. She hired a personal trainer and a nutritionist to get down to the size 6 she always "dreamed of." From an outsider's view, you would swear that Jackie R. was the one getting married—not her sister.

The sad part of Jackie R.'s story was that, while she might have been the perfect sister to her BTB, she wasn't being perfect to *herself*. To accommodate her bride's every need, she had skipped out on two romantic dinners with her boyfriend, cancelled four very important doctor appointments, and handed in a couple of assignments late at work.

Sure, these small missteps don't seem like catastrophes, but Jackie R. surely sacrificed herself—beyond reason—for her bride. A mistake you don't need to make.

Your PBT Says: Figure Out How Fixated You Are—Then Fix It

Now that you've learned from Jackie R. what it means to be gruelingly gripped by your bride, let's get back to what your PBT does best—help you diagnose and treat your condition. To understand your own level of fixation fully, take this quick "How Fixated Am I?" quiz:

"How Fixated Am I? Test" Directions

1. Read each of the statements that follow.

2. Choose an answer without giving it too much thought, and circle either *T* for true or *F* for false for each statement.

3. Count the number of *T*s.

"How Fixated Am I? Test" Questions

1. You started making her a scrapbook of her wedding *before* she was engaged. T F

2. You know the names of each member of the band who will be performing at her wedding: Justin, J.C., Lance, Joey. Oops, wrong band! T F

3. You dated one of them. T F

4. You receive phone calls from her wedding planner—before she calls the bride—with questions about the ceremony. T F

5. You rescheduled your long-awaited weekend away to accommodate her wedding shower. T F

6. You're on a get-slim-quick diet to lose twenty pounds before the big day. T F

7. You purchased a "wedding countdown" calendar for *your-self*. T F

8. You go to bed counting the number of steps she needs to walk down the aisle — instead of sheep. T F

9. You and your Bridezilla can't seem to think of anything else to talk about besides the wedding. Seriously, you've tried and it doesn't work. T F

10. Before accepting the offer for your new, amazing job, you mandated taking two weeks off for *her* big day. T F

"How Fixated Am I? Test" Scoring System

8–10 *T*s: You've got a severe case of wedding obsession.

4–7 *T*s: You're fixated for sure.

1–3 *T*s: You're involved but still have your own life. Good for you, girlfriend!

Bridal Case File #27: Amy H.

This is "The Story of the Pearl Earrings."

To this day, it still begs the question: How can one type of precious stone cause so much strife?

It all began in the spring when Amy H.'s bride sent a casual e-mail to all eight of her bridesmaids, asking them rather politely (for a bride that is!) to purchase pearl earrings to wear at her summer wedding.

Amy H., the bride's BFF since freshman year at Tulane, did as many of us bridesmaids would do — rolled her eyes.

"Couldn't the bride pick something more original?" Amy H. asked herself.

"How much do I need to spend on these?" she wondered.

Using her best Bridal Mode skills, however, Amy H. responded to her bride's e-mail request with, "Of course!" and the quintessential smiley face.

Little did Amy H. know the power of these yet-to-be-found pearl earrings.

Three weeks before her bride's big day, Amy H. began obsessing over the pearl earrings. At work as a physical therapist, she noticed that—while flexing the knees of her elderly patients—she had constant thoughts nagging her to go to the mall and pick out some earrings.

At home with her own fiancé, she just couldn't seem to shake the image of the perfect pearl earrings she needed to find. One night, while they were playfully kissing, the image of pearl earrings lodged itself into her mind and would not leave. She knew something was wrong!

In typical fixation fashion, Amy H.'s compulsions began. She went to Dillard's and looked at five different pairs of earrings. None seemed quite right. She went to Macy's and then to Nordstrom's. She went to a high-end boutique and tried on a couple more. She even went to the jewelry district twice.

"The color is too white."

"The shape is not perfectly circular."

"The backing hurts my ears."

No matter how she tried, she could not find any earrings perfect enough. And the obsession went on up until the day of the wedding. In fact, Amy H. *finally* bought a pair just hours before the ceremony began—as thoughts of the perfect pearl still clouded her head.

After the event, Amy H. realized that she had spent $345 and 153 hours obsessing over these earrings.

Today, now removed from the event, she realized that much of her fixation stemmed from the fact that she felt guilty about what kind of friend she had been to her bride. While the two of them were still close after all these years, she wished that she could have been even closer. She eventually realized that her obsession with the pearl earrings was really her distress over her lack of confidence in their relationship. Maybe finding the perfect earrings would make the relationship perfect.

She also wondered, "After spending a fortune on these silly earrings, will I ever wear them again?"

To this day, she's only worn them once!

Your PBT Says: Get Over It!

"Get over it?—ha!" Your PBT wishes it were that easy.

Wouldn't it be nice if, with the snap of your fingers or the bat of your Chanel mascara-stroked eyelashes, your fixation could disappear. But you learned from Amy H. that, unfortunately for you, ain't nothin' that easy!

There's a bit of therapy we need to undergo to rid you of your freaky fixation. And lucky for you, my client, the next few sections of Stage VI are designed to do just that!

Read on to master the must-know therapies for overcoming your obsession.

Exposure and Response Prevention

When real-life therapists treat their patients for fixation they oftentimes use a technique called Exposure and Response Prevention, or ERP.

I know what you're saying. "Enough with the fancy phrases and silly acronyms!" But look beyond all that for now, my subject, you're about to be cured.

ERP works by exposing patients to hypothetical situations that they might obsess over and then teaches them to respond in a nonobsessive manner. We'll use the same technique to overcome your preoccupation with your bride's wedlock. Let's try it out:

Step 1: Relax. Close your eyes.

Step 2: Try to rid your mind of the many thoughts normally racing through it, as if you were wiping it clean with a window squeegee.

Step 3: Focus on the single thought about your bride that you've been obsessing over the most. For example, is your obsession about:

  ♦ Getting your bridesmaid dress altered correctly?

  ♦ Finding the right hotel accommodations that are close enough to the reception hall?

  ♦ Hoping she will like the crystal vase you bought her as an engagement gift?

  ♦ Wondering if your supercute new boyfriend will get along with her future hubby?

  ♦ Wishing that your hair will look perfectly coiffed on the big day?

Step 4: Imagine your responses to these situations. Now, stop and tone down your responses dramatically—as much as possible. For example, if your obsession is about:

  ♦ Getting your bridesmaid dress altered correctly: Instead of calling for references for the top five seamstresses in your city, be reasonable. Make just one phone call to a friend for a recommendation and book your appointment for a fitting.

  ♦ Finding the right hotel accommodations that are close enough to the reception hall: Instead of spending hours searching on Travelocity.com and Mapquesting the distance between various hotels and the reception, ask your bride which hotel she recommends. Then book it. It's that simple.

♦ Hoping she will like the crystal vase you bought her as an engagement gift: There's no point overanalyzing the potential pitfalls of crystal. Remember, if you bought it, she'll love it. And if she doesn't, trust that she'll be more than happy to return it for something else.

♦ Wondering if your supercute new boyfriend will get along with her future hubby: This obsession may require some work, but do your best not to overthink it. Be certain to plan a couple of casual get-togethers. Perhaps dinner with the two couples first and then golf for "men only." They'll be best buds in no time. And if they're not, so be it.

♦ Wishing that your hair will look perfectly coiffed on the big day: Rather than spend hundreds of dollars getting "practice blowouts" at the top salons in your neighborhood, relax yourself. Make just one appointment at a reasonably priced place. Remind yourself of the reality that folks will really be focused on *her* hair. Yours? Not so much.

Your PBT Says: Separate Bridal Life from Real Life

Now that you've grasped ERP, it's time to tackle another exercise program.

We've all heard the expression, "Work–Life Balance." It's what our boss usually quotes when she needs to take the day off for Ivana's Brazilian bikini wax downtown.

It's time for you to adopt a similar phrase—no painful hair-removal appointment required: "Bride–Life Balance."

Come on—say it with me! Bride–Life Balance. It has a nice ring to it, doesn't it?

Bride–Life Balance (BLB) are the three words you need to

replay in your head, say out loud, or write on a Post-it—whatever it takes to be ingrained in your far-too-fixated frame.

BLB is a friendly way of reminding yourself, your bride, and anyone else who has to deal with your obsession that you recognize the need to separate yourself from the bride.

BLB has some psychological backbone to it, of course. Freud developed a similar process called Individuation. Individuation occurs when someone who was previously too attached to an event or a person finally becomes more independent. Like a baby girl taking her first steps without holding her mommy's hand. Or a woman finally breaking free from a bad relationship.

Live Bride-Life Balance

Now that you've mastered the expression Bride–Life Balance, it's time to start living BLB. It's time to regain your sense of self, sister!

Remember what it feels like to break up with someone? After all the fighting is said and done, you need to remember what *you* like—who *you* are. Same applies here. No fighting or ex-boyfriends needed.

Start with a few tricks of the therapy trade, designed to get you individuating in no time:

Think summer camp. Oh, the joys of youth—like summer camp. Remember the endless activities, such as arts and crafts, soccer, and swimming? Take a moment to remember which activities you liked best back in the day and get back into 'em.

If summer camp programs were not your thing, remember what *was* your thing when you were a girl. Was it writing? Was it painting? Was it ballet dancing? Sign up for a local writing course. Join the local women's basketball team. Why not take those waterskiing lessons you've always wanted to try out? Now's the time to use activities to reactivate yourself!

Plan your own big day. Remember what we learned in Stage V? The bride's not the *only* one who deserves all the fun—you, too, can enjoy the merriment of planning an important day—for yourself, that is.

Maybe it's the day you host a chic dinner party at your new flat. Maybe it's the day you clean out your closet for the first time in five years. Maybe it's the day you'll finally say "hi" to the cute Barista at Starbucks whom you've been eyeing for three months.

Become a Marthaphile. Okay, so I'm not talking about wearing Martha Stewart's dopey sweaters or spending time in the clink. But the woman sure does have a lot to teach when it comes to home decoration!

Use Martha as an inspiration to paint your living room that deep brown shade you've always been a bit afraid of or as motivation to try out that leopard-print duvet cover. In the end, re-decorating your home will feel like you've re-decorated yourself. Just think, everyone needs a little touch-up once in a while!

Ring the bell! The school bell that is. A little learnin' never hurt anyone. Sign up for a continuing education class at the local Y or that online class about The Shifting Dynamics of Latin American Politics. Trust me, your brain will thank you for giving it a bit of much-needed exercise.

Cook good. Feel good. Whether you're a master chef or still struggling to boil water, spending some time in the kitchen can *actually* be good for you. Whether you gain your inspiration from Rachel Ray or from your mom's yellowed recipes, pick a day to master a challenging recipe. Invite your friends or boyfriend over for a tasting. Even if the meat is too tough or the spaghetti too soft, you'll feel great that you actually produced *something* mildly edible.

For inspiration to live BLB, read about Tiffany D.

Bridal Case File #11: Tina D.

Tina D. was the absolute example of what it truly means to achieve BLB.

Just a few years ago, living life as a somewhat successful real estate analyst in her mid-twenties, Tina D. was spending the majority of her time coping with the many weddings she needed to attend.

Weekend after weekend, weddings just seemed to keep popping up. Day after day, more engagements just seemed to be announced, and Tina D. was there—for her friends and family—with bells on every time.

By the time her two-year spurt of weddings had come to a slowdown, Tina D. knew she needed to regain her sense of self—she needed to achieve BLB. And coincidentally, Tina D.'s idea for BLB began to take shape at one of her many wedding events.

While at the Sunday brunch after a posh New England wedding at the Boston Museum of Fine Arts, she stumbled upon the most magnificent Matisse. Never a lover of arts in the past, Tina D. could not stop staring at the masterpiece. The colors grabbed her. The strokes of paint called her name.

At the end of the brunch, she purchased a postcard of the picture and thumbtacked it to her office wall at her stodgy firm.

After a few months of endless gazing at her postcard, Tina D. decided it was time to see what the art world was really about, and she enrolled in continuing education courses at Boston University at night. After nine months of courses, she was ready to do more.

That's right. She quit her job and went back to school for art history. Today she's the assistant curator at one of Newbury Street's most prestigious galleries. What's the lesson to be learned from Tina D.? Achieving BLB can make you as happy as can be!

Your PBT Says: Say a Fond Farewell to Fixation

Now that you've unraveled yourself from your bride's life—and begun to focus rightfully on your own—answer this question honestly: "Are you thinking about your bride right now?"

It is hoped that your answer is a resounding, fixation-free, "No, I have more important things to worry about than my bride, doc!"

If your answer is not quite as crystal clear, you may still have a bit of work ahead of you to rid yourself fully of those fixation follies. So feel free to return to this chapter whenever you need a healthy dose of "get over your bride and get on with your life!"

CHAPTER SEVEN

Stage VII: Family Therapy

Yes, there really *is someone worse*
than your bride

Your PBT Says: Wedding Reality Bites, Baby

Just when you thought you'd seen it all—all the dispensable drama, all the futile fluffiness, all the haphazard hoopla, all the turbulent temper tantrums and near fist fights . . . Just then and only then, it hits you over the head like a chunky, sequined pump, drowning in Bridezilla foot sweat: there is *actually* someone worse than your bride! Her family.

I've shielded you, as any good therapist would, up until Stage VII to keep you focused on the task at hand—surviving your bride. But now that you've learned the techniques to manage her effectively, you're ready for the big leagues, baby. Welcome to Stage VII: Family Therapy.

Stage VII trains you how to cope with this unexpected band of bridal badness—those whom I affectionately refer to as the "Bridal Others": like the monstrous mother of the bride, the ferocious fiancé, or the evil maids of honor.

But don't run and hide! Your PBT will be with you every scary, rice-sprinkled step of the way—or down the aisle—helping you cope with this bunch of bridal beasts.

Your PBT Says: Master the Art of Family Therapy

What's the key to passing Stage VII with flying colors? Taking the psychological high ground! In order to do so, it's time to master another set of therapeutic tactics designed to keep *you* happy — and to keep those intrusive Bridal Others at bay. That's right, my pupil. It's time to learn a bit about Family Therapy.

To start, I'd like to introduce you to Dr. Minuchin, one of the forefathers of family therapy. Go ahead and shake his imaginary hand. It's not like you've got a ring on your finger to get in the way!

Dr. Minuchin believes that the key to effective family therapy is putting the whole entire family — no matter how dysfunctional — in one room. Then shaking things up a bit and seeing what happens. Sounds like fun — well, maybe for the troublemaking Dr. Minuchin!

Unlike regular one-on-one therapy sessions during which the therapist and patient would have a nice chat, Dr. Minuchin's sessions involve moms, dads, siblings, grandparents, and whoever else wants to come along for the therapeutic joyride. In the case of Sparkles the cat, Dr. Minuchin may let her in too.

Why does this mischief-making Minuchin subject his patients to what sounds like forty-five minutes of expensive psychological torture? Because Dr. Minuchin wisely wants to see how the *entire* family — what he calls a "system" — functions as a whole. During his nontraditional group therapy sessions, he looks for patterns in the family's behavior that he believes would occur off the therapist's comfy couch, in the real world.

So what can *you* learn from this rogue of an M.D.? That just like Dr. Minuchin's patients, your bride's crazy family members are not operating in isolation. They are part of a larger unit, what your PBT calls the "Bridal System."

So whether you're dealing with the MOH or the higher-maintenance-than-the-bride-herself groom, these folks are part of a bigger, sometimes maddening, and dysfunctional relationship with the bride. And—right or wrong—that's why these Bridal Others often take out their anger on the innocent victim, pretty little you.

"Great news, doc!" you must be thinking. "First I have to deal with my bride. Now I have to worry about her nutty family too? What's a girl to do?"

The answer, my treasure, is easier than you might think. That's right. The names and faces may have changed, but some things— like Bridal Mode—remain the same. Channeling Bridal Mode is highly effective in helping you deal with nearly every clown in your bride's daft wedding circus. No, you may not be dealing with a Bridezilla in this situation. But, yes, you need to take the same nothing's-gonna-get-me-down stance.

Stage VII provides the specific advice you need to deal with each of the bridal family members who are (un)lucky enough to be part of your bride's "Bridal System." And while your PBT will not put all of 'em in one room as Dr. Minuchin does, I will teach you how to deal with each member individually and successfully.

So the next time one of these Bridal Others tries to take out her wedding frustrations on you—just smile hard. Think positive. Remember, it will all be over soon. And above all, no matter how much drama these wedding party patrons stir up, *you*—and your sanity—*must* remain the priority.

Your PBT Says: Throw Mom-Zilla from the Train!

We all learn so much from our mothers: how to dress, how to speak properly, how to present ourselves to the world, how to treat our friends and family.

In the case of most Bridezillas, your bride likely modeled her my-way-or-the-highway mantras after her mother.

Unfortunately, while you may easily be able to detect what your bride learned from her mother, you may have a harder time diagnosing the dreaded Mom-Zilla. The tricky thing about the Mom-Zilla is that she doesn't present her symptoms outwardly. Only a trained eye can spot the evil that lurks behind her smile or the insecurity inside her as she hugs the wedding guests.

But no matter how sweet this "Mother" seems to be, no matter how complimentary she is of your Banana Republic sheath dress at the engagement party and no matter how much money she spends on your table setting at the wedding, she only cares about one thing: making this wedding the greatest day of her daughter's life. And she's got the power, the purse strings, and the panache to prove it!

To help you accurately spot the ghastly Mom-Zilla from even miles away, read the Top Ten Signs to look out for.

The Top Ten Signs of the Mom-Zilla

10. She is the one who is more likely to ring your phone at 1:00 A.M. in the morning—than the bride would be—to discuss wedding preparations with you.

9. She beamed when the groom asked permission to marry her daughter, and then this same MOB kissed him and hollered, "Thank God! Someone with money is taking her!"

8. She knows each of the bridemaids' cell phone numbers, work numbers, and e-mail addresses. By heart.

7. She opened her own wedding invitation store, just to ensure that she would have the perfect paper selection for her bridal baby.

6. She dropped thirty-six pounds for the big day. More than this MOB did for her *own* wedding.

5. She goes out for lunch with the wedding planner. At least once a week.

4. She quit her day job to focus more time on planning her daughter's wedding.

3. She did not think the bride's ring was quite big enough to meet her high standards so she secretly paid for the groom to add one large baguette on each side.

2. She took out a loan to renovate her Hampton home, just in case out-of-town guests swing by the day after the wedding.

1. She has conference calls with the bridal party to discuss logistics and outstanding topics, every Wednesday at 10:00 A.M.

To understand the Mom-Zilla further in all her glory, read on and learn from Gwen Y's. story.

Bridal Case File #40: Gwen Y.

Gwen Y.'s bride was very calm, very collected, and very much the kind of bride we all wish we could get every time.

The easy-going bride's mom? That was another story!

In fact, the bride's bridezillaness skipped the bride entirely and transitioned fully over to the mother. Unfortunately for Gwen Y., it was not until the bride's mom called Gwen Y. one memorable Wednesday night that she realized who she was dealing with—the Mom-Zilla from hell.

From the moment Gwen Y. said, "Hello?" the Mom-Zilla balled her out for six minutes straight. By the time Gwen Y. managed to get a word in, she realized why this MOB was so crazed.

According to the daffy Mom-Zilla, she had e-mailed Gwen Y. twice over the weekend to confirm her attendance at the upcoming engagement party, but she had not yet heard back from Gwen Y.! The Mom-Zilla had even left Gwen Y. a voice mail on her office line to reach her. Gwen Y.'s lack of response equaled a lack of respect in the Mom-Zilla's eyes. And she let Gwen Y. know it.

Gwen Y. stuck to her guns—and to her Bridal Mode skills— to cope with this manic MOB. Rather than hang up on her as she would have *liked* to do, she calmly responded with the grace and poise of any well-schooled Bridal Therapy student.

"Yes, I realize that you may be upset," Gwen Y. said as she took a deep breath. "But I have been traveling on business for the past few days. Of course I plan to attend the engagement party and appreciate your invitation. Good night."

What lesson can we learn from Gwen Y.? As insane as the MOB's behavior may have been, Gwen Y. did what she was trained to do—respond to one of the Bridal Others with calm, collectiveness, and respect—even if respect was the last thing she really felt. In the end, the MOB apologized to Gwen Y. for her uncalled for phone call. Gwen Y. graciously accepted her apology. Good for you, Gwen Y.!

In addition to remembering to employ Bridal Mode whenever dealing with the dreaded Mom-Zilla, here are three more tips to help you manage her:

1. *Give her a little R-E-S-P-E-C-T, even when you really want to give her something else.* All this woman really wants is to feel respected and appreciated.

   That's because, so very often, the bride does not acknowledge the MOB's support and involvement as much as the MOB would wish. So indulge the MOB. Always be as respectful and gracious as possible when you interact, whether or not you're chatting in person or replying to her wedding invitation.

2. *Be overly polite, even when you want to be crass.* No one loves good manners more than Mom. So remember what your *own* mom taught you. Say "please," "thank you," and "pardon me."

   Most likely the MOB is contributing to the wedding financially in some way, so always express your gratitude for being invited and for being part of the process—even when you wish you weren't!

3. *Be complimentary, even when it kills you.* Again, think about what makes your *own* mom happy: a compliment. Go ahead and tell the MOB how much you love her Talbot's flats or her Chico's jacket that was pieced together in Guatemala. It will make her day and get *you* on her good side. Just think, paying someone else a compliment—even the monstrous Mom-Zilla—always makes you feel better about yourself as well.

Your PBT Says: Get Over the Overly Involved Father of the Bride

Now that you've mastered Mommy Dearest, it's Daddy's turn!

That's right. We all know *this* guy. He's the dad we wish we had: the guy who buys his lovely daughter a Lexus at the drop of a hat, helps her write her dissertation at 2:00 A.M. on any given Sunday, hangs Ikea pictures in her apartment. Even drives twenty miles to her condo to kill the monster-sized water bug perched on her kitchen sink.

He's the dad who drove up for Homecoming Weekend every year at Colgate, who worked from home just to spend more time with the kids, and who *still* pays her phone bills.

So when it comes time for this man's precious princess to get married, get ready to feel his presence even more. He's about to get this girl whatever she wants for her magical day—all expenses, time and logic put aside.

He's the I-Never-Say-No-to-My-Daughter-Father-of-the-Bride. And how do you know if you're dealing with him? Just take this quick quiz. Put a check next to any of the symptoms that sound familiar. If you count more than two check marks, then you've successfully diagnosed a daddy gone bridal!

☐ You've seen *him* more times this month than you've seen your *own* father.

☐ He's so involved in the flower selection and decorating process for the big day that you're starting to question his sexuality.

☐ You've never heard him say "No" to his daughter. Even when he caught the two of you sneaking out of the house at 2:00 A.M. sophomore year of high school.

☐ If there's an emergency, the bride calls her dad *before* she calls her husband-to-be.

☐ The code to disarm this father's family home is the bride's birthday.

☐ She's the only daughter in the family.

☐ He pays the bride more compliments than he does his own wife.

☐ When his daughter totaled the family car, he totally

bought her a new car of her choice within weeks. Complete with leather interior upgrade.

To help you further understand the Overly Involved Father of the Bride, Shirley B. can help.

Bridal Case File #50: **Shirley B.**

Shirley B.'s buxom, blond bride was the only ounce of femininity in a house filled to the brim with testosterone. Just imagine, one dad, three brothers, one sister, one bathroom. The bride's mother had remarried years ago and lived in Tampa with her younger husband, leaving the bride, her dad, and the rest of the male monkeys to rule the primate house.

What did that mean for the BTB? Her dad became involved in absolutely every aspect of her childhood, her adolescence, and her young adulthood. Of course, when it came time to get married? You guessed it. Her dad became more involved in the wedding than the bride herself!

For the destination wedding in Colorado, the father of the bride flew to Aspen nearly every other week to check in with the caterers and check out the mountaintop. He held weekly calls with the decorator. He even hand stuffed and hand stamped the wedding invites all by his lonesome.

Shirley B. thought that his behavior was sweet. In fact, she caught herself green with envy at times. That was until this demonic daddy came down unnecessarily on Shirley B.! After giving what she thought was an eloquent "toast to the happy couple" at the engagement party, Shirley B. was in for a shock.

When the bride's dad asked Shirley B., "Can I speak with you in the other room?" she assumed this dad was going to thank her for her kind words. Instead, he asked her, "Did you give your speech more than five minutes thought before you blurted it out?"

Speechless, Shirley B. did not know how to respond. Instead, this despicable dad continued on, "You had better put some more thought into your wedding night toast or I don't think you'll make the cut as maid of honor."

With that, he walked away, leaving Shirley B. shocked and nearly in tears.

It took her a ton of restraint to hold herself back from crying or from making a scene, but Shirley B. kept her calm. And despite this dad's way-uncalled-for words, Shirley B. went back to the party and enjoyed herself.

After the traumatizing event, Shirley B. kept her distance from dear ole dad. And while she was tempted to tell her bride what a monster he was, she held back, remembering that the wedding can get the best — or the worst — of anyone and everyone. Even the father of the bride.

Take it from Shirley B., sometimes the father of the bride can be too involved for his own good. So if he gets in *your* hair too much, apply the same rules you learned for the MOB. Just add a tad of machismo:

1. *Give him a little R-E-S-P-E-C-T too, just like you did with the MOB.* This is probably not too big of a stretch for a kind soul like yourself. But given that this guy is probably coughing up more than a couple of bucks in the next few months as well as "losing" his daughter to another man, he'll be more sensitive than you'd think. Any ounce of respect you can demonstrate will do wonders.

    Call him "Sir," instead of "Kathy's dad." Arrive on time for all wedding events. Thank him for inviting you to the engagement party, the wedding, and the after-wedding brunch.

2. *Put your manners on full blast.* Just 'cause he's a guy doesn't mean he doesn't appreciate politeness. So the usual "please" and "thank-yous" are a given. But go the extra mile and thank this man for dishing out the cheddar to include you in the wedding—most likely, *he's* the one paying for your sixth glass of chardonnay at the rehearsal dinner!

3. *A little flattery from a female goes a long way.* Try "what a great pair of loafers" or "I love your Brooks Brothers tie!"

    What fifty-plus guy wouldn't love a compliment from a hot twenty-something like yourself? Just remember not to take it too far. You surely don't want him to mistake your compliment for a come-on.

4. *Tell him how much his princess means to you too.* It never hurts to let Daddy know how wonderful his bride is and how much you "heart" her—despite her crazy Bridezilla behavior. So let her dad know, "I love your daughter *almost* as much as you do" or "I am so proud of your daughter— she means so much to me."

Your PBT Says: Step Aside, Bride—Here Comes the Groom!

Just because *she's* the one getting married, doesn't mean *he's* not gonna cop a 'tude! Seriously, in today's metrosexual society, men's rights are changing every day. They, too, are now entitled to the same royal treatment. The same ass kissing. The same manicures and pedicures. And in some cases, the same snotty attitudes as brides.

And just because *they're* not the ones wearing the gowns, doesn't mean they're not ready to raise some matrimonial hell.

In many cases, they are just as demanding, just as stressed, just as detail obsessed—if not more so—than their brides to be. After all, they've got just as many folks to impress, "man jewels" to don, and hair to perfect.

What's the best way to handle the Groom from Hell? Start by remembering what we learned from family therapy—it's not about the individual, but it's about the Bridal System. And if the groom is anything like his Bridezilla, this system is probably pretty broken. Rather than try to fix their relationship, you need to adopt a special version of Bridal Mode—you've got it! Groom Mode:

+ Imagine he's your bride, just a bit hairier.
+ Compliment his outfit, even if it kills you.
+ Ask if he's excited about the big day.
+ Smile big whenever you talk to him. Just make sure he doesn't interpret your kindness for flirtation.

Not sure if you're dealing with a true Groom from Hell? If you answer *T* to two or more of the following statements, it's official. This groom's probably got the devil horns and pitchfork hidden at home to prove it!

1. He spends more time putting "product" in his hair when getting ready for wedding events than the bride does. T F

2. He attends every meeting with the wedding planner. Even when the bride can't make it. T F

3. He is obsessed with the wedding details and has forced you to ask yourself at least once, "Could he be gay?" T F

4. He talks about the wedding more often than the bride does. T F

5. He freaked out last week because the linen for the table settings *still* had yet to arrive from France. T F

6. He spent more for his tux than the bride's wedding dress. T F

7. He has wedding preparations that call for waxing, tanning, and microdermabrasion. That's for him. T F

8. He has reinvested most of his 401K in ordering the perfect roses for the reception area. T F

9. He has far more groomsmen than she has bridesmaids. T F

10. He has dreamed of the wedding day since he was age eleven. Yes, we're talking about the groom. T F

Bridal Case File #5: Delia F.

Delia F. from LA absolutely loved her best friend's fiancé. Friends with the bride since college, Delia F. actually set up the loving couple—after Delia F. had gone out on a date with the future groom to be and decided that her best friend would much prefer this manly, yet metrosexual, man.

Delia F. was right! And the couple had been inseparable ever since. And now that they were getting married, Delia F. knew that the groom would be mighty particular about every teensy, weensy detail.

After all, this was the guy who had four mirrors in his studio apartment strategically positioned to cover every angle of his hair.

This was the guy who referred to himself in the third person as "Benjamin." And referred to his—what shall we say—smaller self as "Big Ben."

This was the guy who spent hours at Fred Segal's selecting the perfect tie, days on Bluefly.com finding the most impeccable shoes, hours standing on line at the local Coffee Bean waiting for the perfect mocha skim Chai, half decaf.

Everything, and I mean everything, had to be just so for this "so fab" LA guy. From the tux to the tablecloth to the tuna tartare to the toasts.

But this Groom from Hell officially went above and beyond "sweating the details" when he commented on Delia F.'s rehearsal dinner dress. She had chosen to recycle a simple, A-line Ann Taylor number. While she'd worn it to a few events in the past, she figured no one would notice—nor would they care—that this dress was a "repeat offender."

Leave it to the way-too-particular groom! When Delia F. greeted the happy couple and kissed the groom on the check, he whispered in her ear, "Don't worry. I won't remind everyone that you're wearing the same dress you wore to college graduation. I know money's tight."

Delia F. couldn't believe her ears—or the fact that this guy remembered the last time she wore the flowered frock. She responded, "Don't worry. I won't remind everyone that you spent more time fixing your hair than your fiancé did tonight. I know how particular you are."

Excellent job dealing with this ghastly groom, Delia F.!

Take it from her, just because he's got a Y chromosome doesn't mean he's not Xtra crazy when getting married.

Your PBT Says: Nothing Bites Harder Than a Bitchy Bridesmaid

Pop Quiz:

What's harder to handle than even the most emotionally disturbed Bridezilla?

Pencils down.

The answer: a fired-up bridesmaid who's been bestowed the bridesmaid title one too many times!

You'd think this girl would have *some* ounce of compassion left in her victimized heart. You'd think she'd be nice to a fellow bridesmaid or friend of the bride, like you. You'd think she'd be happy to welcome you to the unwonderful world of weddings.

Think again.

As much as she hates the wedding process, she's become so much of a bridesmaid that she doesn't know how to stop.

Unfortunately for you, she's likely gaming to get out of this wedding tournament as quickly as possible. And just like the "new girl" at school needs to pay homage to the popular crowd, you too may need to make nice with this owner of the bridesmaid title.

Learn the bridesmaid lesson from Lindsey E., below.

Bridal Case File #21: Lindsey E.

Lindsey E. was one of those women who those of us "in the bridal know" refer to as a freshman. When Lindsey E.'s bride—her big sister from Sigma Kappa at Michigan—asked her to serve as a bridesmaid in her October Fest wedding, Lindsey E. was thrilled. This would be her first time in a wedding party and her first time as a bridesmaid.

"Thank you so much!" Lindsey E. told her bride. "I can't wait!"

Once she met her fellow bridesmaids, however, she realized that she actually could wait. She met the other bridesmaids for the first time when the four of them went bridesmaid dress shopping in chilly downtown Chicago.

Wearing comfy clothes and a captivating smile, Lindsey E. was excited for a fun day out with the girls. But when she met the other bridesmaids, she realized that the chill in the air was not from the Windy City. In fact, cold was not enough to describe their frosty demeanor. Three years older than Lindsey E., they made it known from the start that they were experienced bridesmaids. And boy were they bitter about it!

As they tried on dresses, Lindsey E. asked a few innocent questions. "Does this dress come in other colors?" "Do I have to dye my shoes to match my dress?" "How are you going to wear your hair on the big day?" With every question came a roll of the eyes, a sigh, and a "you are so naïve!" from one of the bitchy bridesmaids.

After four hours of dress shopping with these depressing divas, Lindsey E. better understood what she was dealing with. She was not going to be friends with these girls. She was not going to win.

But like a pro, Lindsey E. accepted things as they were with a smile. She kept her head high, and she kept her Bridal Mode in full effect to keep up with these bridesmaids throughout the entire wedding preparation process.

When attending the series of events leading up to the big day, for example, Lindsey E. was sure to keep her distance from this pack of prickly piranhas. Whether it was at the bridal shower or the bachelorette party, Lindsey E. decided not to go out of her way to strike up a friendly conversation with these sassy sisters.

Sure, they whispered about her handbag color and gap t-shirt behind her back. However, by the time all the vows were said and done, Lindsey E. had graduated from freshman bridesmaid to sophomore, vowing never to treat another fellow bridesmaid the same way these women treated her.

Your PBT Says: Maid of . . . What?

Now that you're prepared to deal with the evil bridesmaid step-sisters, get ready for the stepmother of them all—the MOH.

Today's maids of honor are dealing with the demands of the BTB. And as a result, they're taking it out on the rest of us. So while honor may be in their title, it often gets thrown out the window when they have to deal with the bride.

To understand the maid of—well—$\partial\omega$-honor better, have a read about one of this PBT's worst cases of an MOH gone bad.

Bridal Case File #13: Kristen K.

As the fifth bridesmaid in her older cousin's Atlanta bridal party of eight, Kristen K. was unfortunate enough to be forced to deal with Georgia's least peachy MOH in history.

This so-called Southern belle MOH had *nothing* on even the worst of bridezillas: her demands were insane, her atti-tude unkind, her smile forced.

She made her Bridesmaids do it all. From requiring that they participate in weekly conference calls to ensure that they were staying on track with their bridesmaid duties to man-dating that they handwrite greeting cards of encouragement to the bride during her wedding dress alterations, this MOH was officially out of control And her catchphrase, "Wouldn't you want the bride to do the same for you?" was oh so an-noying!

The night before the wedding, Kristen K. couldn't believe how far the MOH had the gall to go! After finally falling asleep—despite the boisterous sounds from the boys in the next hotel room—the phone sprung Kristen K. out of her delicate sleep. Would this MOH ever stop, she wondered.

Before Kristen K. had a chance to say, "Hello?" the MOH started in.

"Wake Up! It's time to practice!" the MOH said. "The entire bridesmaid party is required to meet in the reception hall downstairs for a mandatory wedding walkthrough! Be there at 3:30 A.M. sharp."

Kristen K. couldn't believe the sass of this Southerner.

Despite the crust in her eyes, the slippers on her feet, and the red wine still rumbling in her belly, she got out of bed and did as the MOH commanded that night.

For two hours, she channeled Bridal Mode as this MOH ensured that each bridesmaid correctly memorized her order in line and practiced the appropriate way to fluff the bride's dress.

When all was said and done, Kristen K. promised herself that — no matter how much she loved her bride — she would never again let an MOH do as this Atlanta diva did.

How do you know if you're dealing with an MOH as dreadful as Kristen K.'s? Circle the *T* or *F* next to each of the following diagnostic answers. If you circled *T* to two or more answers, your MOH is likely to make your wedding experience far from wonderful.

◆ She has not consulted you in planning the wedding shower. She's just planning to send you the bill for your portion. T F

◆ She conveniently "stole" your wedding gift idea and didn't tell you until the day before the bachelorette party. T F

◆ She hangs out with all the bridesmaids and starts her sentences with, "Now, girls, I know from experience..." T F

◆ She e-mailed the wedding party a schedule for dress shopping, shoe shopping, and alterations, without checking their calendars first. T F

◆ She's checked on you twice already today to make sure you're sticking to her schedule. T F

Your PBT Says: Get Ready for the Wedding Planner from Hell

It's one thing to answer to your bride or to her overly anxious mother or to her bizarre bridesmaid, but it's another to answer to a complete stranger—the wedding planner.

Just because she's arranged the flowers, coordinated the table settings, or organized the waitstaff doesn't mean she's suddenly your boss. But watch out, sister, she probably thinks she is!

Inevitably, her name is Cherri or Terri. She wears skirt suits circa 1993. And she's getting paid to do whatever it takes to make the bride happy. For sure she'll do so at *your* expense without a second thought.

She'll advise you on your hairstyle, ask you to put out that "must-have" smoke before walking down the nerve-wracking aisle, and remind you to fix the bride's train. And she'll probably do it with unwarranted attitude.

The best way to deal with these downtrodden divas is to remember that while they need to answer to the bride, *you* do not need to answer to *them*.

Learn from Marina G. about how to manage the world's worst wedding planner.

Bridal Case File #28: Marina G.

Marina G.'s bridal experience was not half bad. Her bride was relatively sane.

As a bridesmaid, Marina G. was happy because her fellow bridesmaids were all friends from high school. Even the groom was pretty darn decent.

All was well and good in Marina G.'s wedding world until she met her bride's wedding planner named Snow. Yes, Snow. In looking back at the event, Marina G. still can't believe that this stranger had such a stormy impact on the big day.

When Marina G. met Snow for the first time, it was the night of the rehearsal dinner. Marina G. had spent two hours driving in rubberneck traffic from Stanford, Connecticut, to New York City. When she arrived at the event a mere five minutes late, the wedding planner let her have it.

"Hello, I'm Snow, the wedding planner. You must be the late Marina."

"Oh, yes," Marina G. replied. "Sorry."

"No problem," Snow said with an obviously fake smile. "Why don't you get in line with the other bridesmaids behind the curtain so no one can see you."

Marina G. did her best not to take the chilly Snow's remarks to heart. But when this overly obnoxious wedding planner repeated her rudeness the next day at the wedding, Marina G. had enough!

As the bridesmaids primped and prepared for their collective walk down the aisle, they debated about whether to wear their hair back, as the bride requested. Marina G.'s freshly cut bob was just too short to tie back.

She told her fellow bridesmaid, "I hope the bride is okay with me wearing my hair down."

Snow caught wind of this insolence and immediately interjected herself into the previously private conversation. "So, Marina, you're the troublemaker of the group aren't you?"

Marina G.'s mouth was wide open with shock. "Who in the world does this woman think she is?" she said to herself.

"You were late yesterday. And today you want to wear your hair down." She paused and examined Marina G.'s hair. "Well, you have to pin back your bangs. No way is the bride gonna allow this!"

Rather than respond with equal rudeness, Marina G. channeled the Bridal Mode she had practiced from other wedding experiences. She calmly told the world's worst wedding planner, "It is up to the bride. I will discuss this with her, not you."

Actually, Marina G. ended up pinning her bangs back but only at the bride's express request.

And in the end, the wedding was a wonderful memory for Marina G., except for the blustery wedding planner.

Your PBT Says: Beware, the Wedding-Phobic Man

"Give me a break!" That's what you'll be yelling at your boyfriend/hubbie/fiancé—no matter how super cute he is—when you realize that your usually understanding, sensitive man has become a wedding-phobic little child.

That's right. While the bride typically has an impact on her direct relatives, don't be surprised if she also impacts your man. Learn from Kristie H.:

Bridal Case File #33: Kristie H.

Kristie H. had the sweetest sweetie in all the land: writing her love poems, singing her to sleep, delivering sushi to her when she needed to work late.

But when it came to attending weddings, this consistently kind creature magically transformed into a flaky freak.

Kristie H. realized this when she first began talking to her boyfriend about an upcoming wedding for a high school friend, and he changed topics instantly. When the wedding date approached and Kristie H. tried to make hotel arrangements, her man was beyond disinterested. He was testy. He seemed angry. He seemed bitter.

All of a sudden she was "taking him away from the city for the weekend." She was "occupying all his time."—at least according to him.

And on the day of the wedding, as she was getting her hair and nails done with the BTB, her boyfriend called to say he was too sick to attend. "But you've already RSVPed. They've planned and paid for you."

After much back-and-forth, Kristie H. finally persuaded her man to forgo the ceremony but at least attend the reception. She nearly had to pull some teeth to get him there.

So, how should *you* manage your potentially wedding-phobic man? You need to realize that these feelings of avoidance and even anger stem from very strong emotions.

Maybe this guy fears commitment. In fact, his wedding phobia may be a watchout. His not wanting to attend a wedding may mean that he doesn't want to attend a wedding with *you*. But don't panic. If you're meant to be together, you'll survive this stage. If not, you'll find another man who can deal with a wedding and more importantly, a wedding with you.

It is also critical to know that these guys—scared silly of weddings—may also be terrified of impressing your friends and family. Oftentimes, your man may fear having to make conversation with your Aunt Lidia, dance the Hora with your dad, or wait two hours by himself for you to finish taking wedding party pics.

Of course, the worst part of it all for him is what your PBT refers to as the "wedding waiting game." This game is played when you're in the wedding party and he's not. So when it's time for you to get your hair done with the bridal party, he waits. When it's time for you to walk down the aisle, he waits. When it's time for you to take pictures with the wedding party, he waits.

Let's face it. This likely ain't fun. So cut him a bit of slack if you think he deserves it. Either way, you're officially forewarned and prepared to prevent your man from letting the wedding get the worst of him.

Your PBT Says: Learn How to Manage Your *Own* Mom

Nothing brings out the worst in our mothers like a little friendly competition — the "*My* Daughter's Getting Married" competition, that is.

Oftentimes, our mothers see so much of themselves in us. We have the career they always wanted. The stick-straight hair they wish they could have achieved with Japanese straightening. The clothes from Barney's they could never afford when they were our age.

So when it comes time for your circle of friends to tie those knots, your mom is waiting with baited breath to see when you'll finish the race. And if you ain't first — she's waiting to see how quickly thereafter you'll follow.

While most of our moms lived through — and even fought for — women's lib — there is oftentimes a hint of an old-fashioned, pre-1960's belief system hidden somewhere inside them. They want to know that you'll be taken care of. That someone will make you happy forever. For some, that they can finally stop paying your rent.

So how do you survive your own mother during your wedding filled stage of life? With a smile! — and with these three simple rules:

> *Rule #1: You are your own woman.* It sounds simple, but it's so true. No matter how much you emulate your mother, and no matter how closely you subscribe to her ideals, you are your own person who makes your own decisions.

If you decide to wait until you're forty-five to get married—or to never get married at all—do what makes you happy.

If you decide to marry rich or to marry poor—or to marry without a care about money in the world—do what makes you happy.

Sure, it may be hard to put aside your mother's strong point of view. But the person you choose to date, the person you choose to marry, and the way you choose to live is 100 percent up to you.

Don't lose sight of who you are—and how you're different from your mother—especially when your mom's wedding clock keeps on ticking.

Rule #2: All your mom wants is to see you happy. Sure, it may be challenging to remember this when your mother's nagging turns into suffocation or when she sends you weekly e-mail reminders to get your ring finger sized or when she threatens to post her own version of your profile on match.com. But cut her some slack. She's only looking out for that elusive thing she wants for you—to see you happy.

Rule #3: Speak your mind. While every ounce of your being does everything possible not to lose your temper or get frustrated by your mother's wedding reminders, you owe it to yourself—and to her—to tell her how you feel. If she's truly getting to you, take a moment to sit her down, tell her calmly how you feel, and give her a hug.

In the end, letting your frustrations fester will only make you feel worse. Just take it from Sally Anne P., speaking your mind can save your relationship with your mother!

Bridal Case Example #9: Sally Anne P.

From the moment Sally Anne P. graduated from Texas A&M, her mom was on a quest. Not to help Sally Anne P. start a successful career or to help her make new friends in Dallas. Her mother's quest was one like no other—to find the perfect husband for her perfectly single daughter.

Although nearly all of Sally Anne P.'s friends were already married or engaged to Southern gentlemen from college, her mother had never before uttered a word about Sally Anne P. getting married.

Now that the reality that Sally Anne P. had graduated with honors—but without a ring—had sunk in, Sally Anne P.'s mother transformed herself into a new woman. A woman on a mission.

At first, this quest didn't bother her. Sure, it was a bit annoying to answer her mother's constant questions like "How is your love life?" or "When is your next date?" But the Southern charmer never let it get to her. That was until the "moving-day incident."

While helping her daughter move boxes into her new Dallas condo, Sally Anne P.'s mom spotted a thirty-something male down the hall. She instantly dropped the box labeled "cheerleader memorabilia" and sprinted toward him as if they were friends.

"Hello, my name is Victoria. Do you live here?" her mother asked the stranger.

"Yes, I do," he replied.

"Well, you just have to meet my eligible daughter who lives down the hall from you."

The next thing Sally Anne P. knew, she was being summoned to the end of the hall to meet this complete stranger— already earmarked as her future husband.

Embarrassed by her mother's behavior and by her own

tattered jeans and sweaty tank, Sally Anne P. reluctantly shook his hand, said a short "Hello," and quickly dashed back to finish moving the boxes her mother abandoned.

"Well he looks like a very nice man," Sally Anne P.'s mother began when she returned to her daughter's new apartment. "I hope he calls," she paused, "because I gave him your number."

"Mama, you cannot decide who I date and when I date. I know you got married when you were eighteen—and that most of my girlfriends are married— but I am not you and I am not them. I want to spend time on my own before you start picking out husbands for me."

And with that, Sally Anne P.'s adventurous mother abandoned her quest—at least for the moment.

Your PBT Says: It Could Be Worse!

Now that you've met this cast of dysfunctional characters, you understand the rule of any and every wedding experience—there is always someone worse than the bride. And now that you've learned the ins and outs and the goods and the bads of the Bridal Others, you're more than ready to take 'em on!

Just remember, even though your life may be a bit more difficult because you have to deal with a type A bridesmaid or bitchy groom, it sure could be a lot worse. At least they're not *your* family!

CHAPTER EIGHT

Stage VIII: Catharsis

*How to create Wedding Well-Being
on the big day*

Your PBT Says: Yippee—I'm Free!

Graduating college with a 3.56 GPA. Presenting the final slide of your masterful PowerPoint presentation at work. Even finishing that extra-sweaty Hot Yoga class without passing out. No matter how lofty—or ordinary—your goal, there's nothing quite like the feeling of finally saying, "I'm done!"

The same holds true when your bride *finally* takes that long-awaited walk down the aisle. Sure, it may be *her* accomplishment, but it is also yours.

You're finally free from your bride's diamond-adorned paws, free from the insane requests, free from prepping and celebrating *her*, and free and ready to move on to way more important things—like you! Your PBT refers to this incredible moment as Wedding Catharsis.

"Cath—what?" you say.

"Catharsis!" Come on, say it with me! "Ca." "Thar." "Sis."

To understand catharsis fully, we'll turn to the man who coined the phrase, Greek philosopher Aristotle. He defined catharsis as an emotional cleansing or climax filled with overwhelming feelings of pity, joy, or extreme change.

Boy, oh boy! Didn't this Greek go-getter get it right? Sure, Aristotle may not have had your future Mrs. in mind when he coined the term. But the sense of release and relief he described certainly applies to your—and to many a—bridal situation.

For those of us coping with the ugly bridal species, Wedding Catharsis is very similar to Aristotle's brand of catharsis. Wedding Catharsis is that climactic moment in which all your wedding energy, anxiety, frustration, and stress finally—and I mean *finally*—culminate. Sure, this turning point may seem impossible to imagine, but give it a whirl.

Close your eyes for a minute. Imagine the day, the moment, the instant when this dreaded wedding day is done. The day when all your jealousy toward the beautiful bride, all your resentment toward the bratty bridesmaids, all your worry about whether your hair will hold up for the 99-degree ceremony will fade away into a distant memory.

Can you picture it? Good girl!

Lucky for you, there's usually more to your Wedding Catharsis than just experiencing it at the end of the wedding journey. There is also the benefit of looking forward to it. That's right. Oftentimes, the key to getting through the entire wedding process— all nine stages—is to imagine exactly what your Wedding Catharsis will be. Then, picture this glorious moment in your head. Trust me, it will keep you motivated, as you fluff her dress yet again, as you make nice to Uncle Harry sitting next to you at your table, and as you even suck in your tummy to fit into another cocktail dress.

SHE'S GONE BRIDAL!

Your PBT Says: Know *Your* Wedding Catharsis!

Now that you understand a bit about what our Greek philosopher friend, Aristotle, had in mind about catharsis, it is time for *you* to define your own, personal Wedding Catharsis. Ask yourself, "What is *my* Wedding Catharsis?"

- When the groom lifts the $500 veil to see her face?
- When the band strikes the last chord at the reception?
- When you clear your throat to end a nerve-wracking wedding toast?
- When you catch the tulip-filled, prized bouquet?
- When you breathe fresh air for the first time after stepping outside of that Long Island banquet hall?
- When you finally take off — and throw away — that hideous bridesmaid dress once and for all?
- When you take a bite of crisp bacon at the morning brunch the day after the event?

Once you have defined your Wedding Catharsis, take a moment to imagine how it will truly feel. Imagine the frown lines instantly disappear from your face. Feel the sweat in your palms dissipate. Touch the soft, non-bridesmaid dress fabric against your skin. Can you imagine it?

If your answer is "Yes, PBT, yes!" then you're on your way to the end of this long, windy, and wicked wedding excursion. Moreover, the vision of your Wedding Catharsis will become your go-to remedy whenever the end seems oh too far away.

That's exactly what our next case example, Stella V., did.

Bridal Case File #3: Stella V.

For Stella V., preparing for her older sister's small, intimate wedding was a large pain in the rear. Yet the biggest pain in the process was surprisingly not her sister. but her mother. From the day the bride announced her engagement to the family, Stella V.'s mother got on her younger daughter's case about her weight like no one's business. Sure, Stella V. would love to drop a few pounds. After all, as a sophomore in college, late-night Domino's orders and her title as "Keg Stand Princess" had helped her pack on and keep the freshman fifteen like the rest of us.

Despite her mother's relentless pursuit to push Stella V. to squeeze into a size 8 bridesmaid's dress, Stella V. knew her mother was being unrealistic. During the dress fitting, Stella V. channeled Bridal Mode. She simply turned to her frantic mother and told her, "Mother, this is the size that I am and I am happy with how I look."

But, no matter how self-assured Stella V. was, she still sought the approval of her weight-obsessed mother. And it was not until the day of the wedding—when Stella V. donned her size 10 dress with confidence and faced her mother— that her divine moment of Wedding Catharsis occurred.

"You look absolutely amazing!" Stella V.'s mother told her emphatically.

"Thanks, Mom," Stella V. said calmly.

And although the bride had yet to walk down the aisle, Stella V. sighed the deepest sigh and smiled the biggest smile she had in the past year. The stress, agony, and pain were over. Now all she had to do was get her sultry size 10 self to the wedding and celebrate her sister!

Your PBT Says: Get Coordinated, Baby Cakes

Now that you're ready to live out your Wedding Catharsis, you still have a few things you must do to prepare for it. As you've learned throughout the past few stages, there's a lot of prep work entailed in getting you and your bride ready for the big day. Particularly during the last few days leading up to the "I do's," there's a ton to keep track of and stay on top of. That's why your PBT has created this handy-dandy Wedding Well-Being Checklist that follows. Take a moment a few days before the wedding day to ensure that you're set and ready to go. Just ask yourself each question in the list. If you can honestly put a "check" next to each question, then you're on track for smooth wedding-day sailing.

Wedding Well-Being Checklist

✓ Do all bridesmaids have their dresses and shoes ready to go for the big day? Is your dress—most importantly—tailored and pressed?

✓ Has the groom finalized the honeymoon plans?

✓ Have you picked up your wedding gift to present to her on the big day?

✓ Have you called the bride today to check in to see how she's feeling?

✓ Have you confirmed your hotel reservations for the weekend?

✓ Has your date dry-cleaned his suit or gotten his tux for the big day?

✓ Have you checked the weather to see how the humidity might affect your hair that day?

✓ Did you pack your suitcase for the wedding and for the brunch the morning after, if necessary? Did you make sure to include aspirin and H_2O in case of a hangover the next morning?

✓ Did you edit your toast and rehearse it out loud at least once?

✓ Did you check in with the groom to make sure he's all set?

✓ Did you clear any days off with your nagging boss?

✓ Did you get the requisite mani, pedi, and bikini wax from Svetlana?

Your PBT Says: Get Psyched Up the Day *Before* the Wedding

Take it from your PBT: the day *before* the big day is nearly as critical as the big day itself. Hard to believe, but true.

Think of the day before the wedding as the calm before the storm, the last day of vacation before going back to work, the massage before the eyebrow wax, the honeymoon before the divorce.

It is your time to relax, unwind, and prepare for the enormous day ahead of you. But all too often, many of us do not take advantage of the day *before*. Rather, the day before is relegated to a day of anxiety and anticipation—not a day of rest and relaxation, which your PBT strongly advises.

To help you prepare for the day *before*, your PBT consulted several veteran bridesmaids for their expert tips on how to take advantage of the day before—and how to get yourself psyched up for the nightmare ahead.

Take Some Time—Even If It's Twenty Minutes—For You

According to our veterans, it is critical to spend some quality time with you know who? You!

After all, you'll be spending the next few days with more people than you're pretty little head may be able to handle and shaking hands with more strangers than you'd like. So take a longer lunch break. Leave work early. Fill up this extra time by strolling for a few minutes in the park, taking a drive in your car, or reading even a few chapters of your new book. Whatever it takes to get yourself alone.

Indulge Yourself

Yes, treating yourself is a tip your PBT has frequently offered throughout your unhappily-ever-after bridal adventure. Our experts also swear by it. Take it from bridesmaid Alexia P., who told me, "No matter how much money I have left in my pocket after all the wedding expenses, I always find a way to get to my favorite salon for some much-needed beauty indulgence the day before the wedding."

According to Alexia P., it's critical that you do the same. The day before the big day, do whatever it takes to get yourself over to your favorite spa or salon. Go for a manicure, pedicure, facial, or blow-dry. If funds are running low—as they often are when financing the prep for Bridezilla's wedding—treat yourself to an at-home mask or mini-microdermabrasion. Your skin will sparkle with relaxation on the big day. And you'll feel like a million bucks even if you didn't spend that much!

Take a Bridal Break

And, boy, will you need one! By the time you reach Stage VIII, you will have spent more hours with—and more money on—your bride than you could have ever imagined. The day before the big day is the perfect time to get some much-needed space from the bridal monster.

Take at least a couple of hours to get yourself physically away from the bride—even if it means you need to turn your cell phone off and leave your BlackBerry at home for just a bit. According to Felicia F., "You'll need some bride-free time without her—I know *I* did!"

Eat Something Yummy

This idea may seem counterintuitive. After all, you've likely been eating healthy—at least skipping the second serving of BK—and sneaking in a tad bit of exercise to fit into your dress as perfectly as possible. But one little treat never ruined anyone's figure. So go on ahead and treat your bridal-loving self to your favorite dessert—whether its Häagen Dazs Double Coffee Twirl or Star-buck's Double-Whipped Chocolate Caramel Mocha! You deserve it.

Replace the Negative with the Positive

As the big day nears, you'll surely be a bit stressed—even though you're not the one getting married. But, according to our expert, Lisa K., "The most important thing is to stay positive. Keep re-minding yourself that it will soon be over!"

Great advice, Lisa K! Just remember, you're almost there. Stay as upbeat and positive as possible—not only for the anxious bride—but, more importantly, for yourself!

Calm Yourself

That's right. For many of us, the day before the *big* day can mean *big* nerves. But that doesn't mean your anxiety needs to get the best of you. Do whatever you can to stay calm and collected. Remember, the calmer you stay, the calmer your bride will be.

Bust out a soothing cup of Chamomile tea. Go for a fifteen-minute massage at the local mall. Take a yoga class at Equinox.

Do whatever you can to stay calm. Trust your PBT, your calmed nerves and clear head will surely come in handy on the big day!

Your PBT Says: Know How to Prep on the Big Day

The big day is actually here.

Just think, within the next twenty-four hours, she'll be walking down the aisle. And—thank goodness—you'll be walking out the door and on your way home!

What's the key to ensuring that today runs as smoothly as possible? Staying as organized as possible. While there is only so much you—as the bride's go-to girl—can do, make sure you do it! Just take it from our bridal champ, below.

Bridal Case File #42: Britney Y.

While Britney Y.'s bride was revving herself up to take her vows on the wedding day, Britney Y. was practically ramping up to call it quits! Truly, this experience had been exhausting, from 4 A.M. on the day the bride called Britney Y. to announce her engagement to 9:00 A.M. on the day of the wedding when the bride began balling over the run in her panty hose.

What kept Britney Y. from fleeing it all and becoming a runaway *friend* of the bride? Staying organized!

As a personal assistant for a wealthy Upper East Side society type in Manhattan, Britney Y. knew what it took to manage the unmanageable—always stay more on top of your game than your client. And, in this case, Britney Y. needed to stay more on top of her game than her bride.

Britney Y. had practically mapped out every minute of every hour—even more so than the bride had. As each hour of the big day progressed, along came Britney Y. ready to check off every detail on her checklist and keep the bride on task.

In the end, Britney Y. kept her calm and her poise, all thanks to a healthy helping of organization and proactiveness. Read on and learn some of Britney Y.'s best kept secrets.

Your PBT Says: Memorize Your Wedding Day Agenda

Your PBT and Britney Y. recommend that you review this hour-by-hour, minute-by-minute Wedding Day Agenda.

7:00 A.M.: Wake up. Call the bride. Ask her if she needs anything, and see how she's feeling. If she's not ready to fly down the aisle, do your best to give her the required pep talk and to calm her nerves—even if you have to fake it a tad. Remind her how special this day is. Refresh her memory that she and her hubbie to be have found each other and are committing to a life of love.

8:00 A.M.: Get in some Bridal Exercise. Take the bride for a jog around the park to get her—and more importantly your—body energized and ready to go. If the bride is not willing to go with 'ya, bring along some of your fellow bridal friends. The fresh air and movement in your legs are bound to give you the pep in your step you need to stay energized throughout the day.

9:00 A.M.: Don't forget to eat breakfast. We all know that breakfast is the most important meal of the day. So on the most important day of her life, don't skimp on the Wheaties. Seriously, whether it's the breakfast of champions or some yummy Yoplait and granola, take a minute to enjoy a tasty A.M. treat.

10:00 A.M.: Get your date ready. If you and your
date/husband/boyfriend are staying at a hotel together,
make sure he has his eyes open, he's showered and
shaved, and he's ready to go.

If you're planning to get ready with your fellow bridesmaids or friends, arrange plans to meet your man at least
fifteen minutes before the ceremony is scheduled to begin.
Remember, when you're dealing with the male species,
you need to account for extra time. Make sure he's got
your cell phone on speed dial in case he needs to reach
you before the big event.

And last but not least, say "Thank you." Sure, you're
the one who truly deserves all the gratitude right now,
but *he's* likely put up with a lot of not-so-fun wedding
drama in the past few months.

11:00 A.M.–2:00 P.M.: Primp and prepare. These next few hours
should be used to get you—and the bride—looking your
bridal best. First don't forget to wear a button-down shirt
today so that it slips off and you can put your dress on
without messing up your freshly done makeup and hair.

The key to managing the next few chaotic hours is
your taking care of yourself first. That's right. You can't
help the bride unless you've helped yourself first. So
manage yourself, your dress, your hair, and your makeup
first. Once you're ready to go, then and only then can
you lend a capable hand to the bride.

Next, it's time to help her. She'll need you for critical
decisions like which shade of fuchsia lip gloss to wear
and which way to part her hair. Once she's got her face
and hair on, it's time for the key event: getting the dress
on. Usually, this is truly a group project that requires ten

or so women just to get the bride into her dress. One foot at a time is always the best rule.

Last, no matter how cheesy the dress, how overdone the makeup, how unchurch-like the cleavage, look her dead in the eye and tell her, "You are a beautiful bride."

2:00 P.M.—Wedding Bells: Before you head out the door, take a few minutes to pack the critical items that will make today as easy and breezy as possible. Check off each item on the list below—and you're good to go!

- [ ] Pepto-Bismol
- [ ] Bobby pins
- [ ] Hairbrush
- [ ] Hairspray
- [ ] Inhaler
- [ ] Hair elastics
- [ ] Directions to the ceremony
- [ ] Bride's cell phone
- [ ] Tampons
- [ ] Comfy shoes
- [ ] Band-Aids
- [ ] Advil
- [ ] Clear nail polish
- [ ] Tic Tacs
- [ ] Clear deodorant

- [ ] Lipstick
- [ ] Double-stick tape
- [ ] $50 in cash
- [ ] Cell phone charger

Your PBT Says: Make the Most of Wedding Mania

Now that you have your game face on, get ready for the craziest few hours you've ever experienced.

There will be tears. There will be laughter. There will be old uncles in far too tight suits. There will even be a 1980s-style, dreaded conga line in which the bride's thirteen-year-old cousin tries to cop a feel.

Yes, my patient, the next few hours of your life may be wacky, may be cheesy, and may even be miserable. But that doesn't mean you can't use the next few abominable hours to your every advantage.

That's right. Little did you know, my cherub, that there actually are some benefits to the bridal bash. Read on so that you, too, can make the wedding day work for you. After all, while her wedding day was designed to bring the husband and wife together, it can bring you some good as well.

The Top Eight Secret Benefits of **Her** *Wedding*

1. Networking is allowed—and encouraged—at the wedding. Just because you're not wearing a power suit or schmoozing with your boss's boss's boss, doesn't mean you can't take advantage of the potential high rollers and influencers at the party. Sure, it may require drinking with the father of the bride's somewhat slimy friends twice your age. Yeah,

you may have to make conversation with strangers. But you're an outgoing, intelligent woman, so give it a try!

Bridal Case File #7: **Molly B.**

That's exactly what Molly B. did at her boss's wedding. While she quite disliked her boss, Molly B. knew that attending the event would be a once-in-a-lifetime chance to toast glasses with the muckety mucks at her company.

And boy was she right! That night she spoke with her mentor for over forty-five minutes, giving her a chance to get her name out there and to get a bit more inspired for work.

Molly B. even took a few minutes to speak with the bride's friends about a new investment opportunity. At one point in the evening, she conducted her own impromptu focus group at two separate tables. She actually used their input to develop her very own invention on the side. To this day, she credits the wedding day experience—and the folks she schmoozed with—for helping her begin her second career as a bona fide entrepreneur.

---

2. Eat. A lot. Seriously, you've likely starved your already perfect frame to fit into that dress for the past three weeks. It's time to put away the Weight Watchers' points, throw away your carb counter for the night, and enjoy some much-needed nutrients. In fact, given that you'll likely be drinking quite a few bubbly beverages tonight, eating may be the smartest thing you can do to ensure that alcohol is in its rightful place—your tummy.

3. Go on, meet Mr. Right! Or even Mr. Right *Now*! Of course, you already know that weddings are notorious for inspir-

ing women to get it on with their fellow wedding guests. But why be ashamed of it? It's time we all embrace the hint of desperation in the air.

There's nothing wrong with flaunting your truly fabulous frame, expertly done makeup, and beautifully coiffed hairdo to help you land a hottie tonight. Remember, just because you're at a wedding doesn't mean you have to marry the guy. If he's cute, if you've had a few drinks, then your PBT grants you access!

That said, there are those of us who take weddings, well, very literally. Those of us, like Beverly S., who like to use the wedding to meet the man whom we'd actually want to, gulp, marry.

Bridal Case File #48: **Beverly S.**

Beverly S. knew she had found her future hubby before he even turned around from his full plate of medium-rare surf and turf. The bride had described Rick S. to Beverly S. — then Beverly K. — a few months before the event — Penn undergrad, Cornell B-school, Goldman Sachs trading desk.

Enough said. Beverly S. was ready — with barren ring finger — to say "I do" as soon as he turned around to shake her hand.

From the moment the bride introduced the two to the moment they took to the dance floor to the moment Rick S. took Beverly K. back to his hotel room, it was wedding day destiny. Today the formerly Beverly K. is now proud to call herself Beverly S. and happy to thank her bride for the critical introduction.

---

4. Sing along with all your high school friends to "Sweet Caroline." Seriously, go ahead. No matter how tone deaf you are—one of the benefits of any wedding is the chance to catch up with your old friends and family.

Take it from your skillful PBT, as we get older, we start to see our friends less and less. It's not as if we can knock on the next dorm room door to greet our best friends these days. With all our crazy schedules and hectic lives, weddings are often the single-best location to bond with our old high school buddies and college gal pals. So don't be afraid to take advantage of this time to move some chairs around, get up and walk to the table or even slow dance inappropriately with your old high school flame. If you want to go the extra mile, request the tried and true "That's What Friends Are For." You'll have so much fun dancing and singing along, you might even forget how dreadfully cheesy the song truly is.

Bridal Case File #4: Olivia P.

Olivia P. really took advantage of her time with her old buddies at a recent event that felt more like a University of Maryland reunion than a wedding. Over twenty sorority sisters and fraternity brothers showed up for the grand fiesta, including Olivia P.'s old beau from freshman year. The two had dated for two years until Olivia P. decided to study abroad in fabulous Florence.

The pair—who had not spoken in over seven years—picked up right where they left off, almost as if they were at the Delta Delta sorority sock hop. The pair danced their sock hop socks off the entire night, and they are still dating to this day.

---

5. Dance your ass off. Seriously, how often do you get to dance to the great tunes of Madonna and Billy Joel? If you've been attending dozens of weddings every year, that chance may come more often than you'd hope. But that doesn't mean you shouldn't enjoy this time to get down and dance, dance, dance! Get out there and practice what "Dancing with the Stars" taught you: technique is not important. Only shaking your butt and having fun are required.

This is also a fab-O time to practice some moves with your date. Take advantage of this opportunity to get out there and take *him* for a spin. Or if you're a single Chiquita, find a cutie at your table and take him for a ride on your dancing train.

6. Become a wedding connoisseur. Sure, wine is a lot more intoxicating than most weddings. But the two have a lot more in common than you thought: the more you sip—or the more you attend—the more you learn what you like and what you don't. It's true, as a veteran wedding attendee, you have a serious advantage over other lucky ladies when it comes to planning your big walk down the aisle someday. By attending all these weddings and checking out all the details, you can mine what you like, criticize what you don't, make jokes about the table arrangements, and determine how they could have done better. That's exactly what our case example, Parker Z., did.

Bridal Case File #10: Parker Z.

At the nine weddings Parker Z. attended before her own, she created a list of all the bands, venues, and florists she liked and those that she didn't. When her turn came a knockin', rather than scramble, she merely opened up her wedding notebook filled with her favs. She realized that flattery — even outright copying — is the best compliment.

7. Gossip, girl. Nothing beats a great wedding when it comes to gossiping about your friends and your family: what they wore, what they didn't, who they brought as their dates, who they didn't, what they ate, what they didn't.

So go on and gossip, girl!

8. Force your boyfriend to catch the garter belt. Weddings are a great chance to get to know how your man *really* feels about you. It's your opportunity to monitor his every movement closely to see what he really thinks about you. Observe how thrilled — or not — he is to be your date. See if he wells up when the bride and groom take their vows. And of course, when the groom throws the garter belt out to all the single men in the room, see how he handles the situation. Does he dive for it like a seasoned baseball player? Or does he cower in the corner, avoiding it like the plague? Be on the lookout, and by the end of the night, you'll have a better sense of what your man thinks about your future together.

Your PBT Says: Put the Bride Aside!

The wedding bells have rung. The bouquet has been tossed. The rice has been thrown. And the "I do's" have been mumbled with tears. Now that it's all said and done, *you're* done!

It's time, my dear, to rejoice in your own private Wedding Catharsis — whatever moment that may have been or whatever time of day in which it may have occurred. However relieved you may have felt, put the bride aside — it's *your* time for relief, relaxation, and celebration.

Stage IX: Withdrawal

What's a girl to do when . . .
gasp . . . the invitations stop coming?

Your PBT Says: Learn How *Not* to Freak When You Wake Up in Non-Wedding Reality

What's guaranteed to be *the* most traumatizing event this year? No, not the season finale of "Desperate Housewives." Nope, not the comeback of Brit-Brit. Nah, not even the return of high-waisted jeans. The most horrific moment will be the day the weddings die.

This is the day you swore on your Juicy Couture sweats would never come. The day you just couldn't imagine.

Just think, no more black-tie weddings *every* Saturday evening. No more engagement parties *every* Friday night. No more wedding showers *every* Sunday at the crack of I'm-way-too-hung-over-for-this dawn.

Alas, the unimaginable day has finally arrived. The truth is ready to be told.

There are no more stiff wedding invitations in your mailbox. There aren't any cheesy bachelorette party evites in your inbox. And—it's true—there are no more wedding items on Bloomingdale's registry waiting to be gifted to yet another not-so-deserving bride.

At first, the mere thought of living in non-wedding reality can be described with only three words: Thank. Freakin'. Goodness!

"Yes!" you scream out loud to your co-workers.

"I have been waiting three years for this day!" you tell your boyfriend.

"Hallelujah!" you text your mom.

But—and there's a big but here, sweetie. Just as every great honeymoon comes to an end, so too may your fleeting moment of joy turn quickly into unexpected panic. It's the panic that comes only when you realize that, sadly, your wedding well has officially run dry.

The day you realize that your weekends now need to be filled with something other than dancing with your Uncle Marty at your cousin's wedding, that your time spent online looking for the perfect mauve strappy sandals now needs to be filled with other activities, that you need to find a new hobby beyond searching for the right clutch to go with your black Betsey Johnson.

For us unmarried gals, it's the day you realize that all your friends are now married off and living happily ever after in suburban McMansions—and that you're still as single as George Clooney.

It's the day you ask yourself, "Why am I the last one left standing, without a sparkler on my finger?" "Why has everyone—but *me*—accomplished what has suddenly become so critical to the once-proudly-single, independent women of the world?"

For married women, the day is equally as traumatizing. Although you were just sick to death of preparing for and attending wedding, after wedding, after wedding, it was actually kinda fun to be part of the "in" wedding crowd. It was exciting to swap horror stories about "do *not* playlists" and wedding planner nightmares. But now that everyone you know is married and hiding away in the burbs all you've got left is, well, your dopey husband at home.

Regardless of whether you're (un)happily single or wed, what you've all got in common on this dreaded day is a flurry of questions running through your head: "What the heck am I gonna do with my time *now*?" "Who am I really? If not the supportive friend or the eternal bridesmaid or the wedding hook-up queen?" "Now that I don't have to spend all my time helping other people get married, what in the world will I do with my non-wedding self?"

Your PBT Says: Diagnose Wedding Withdrawal

As your bridally barren brain fills up with these questions, it's time to face the music — this time without the cheesy cover band. That's right. It's the official end of your wedding whirlwind. And now that your once endless string of weddings has come to a screeching halt, you may be left severely traumatized and feeling incapable of functioning in your non-wedding world.

Don't worry, my pretty. Your PBT has a name and a solution for this devastating event: diagnosing you with Wedding Withdrawal — or WW.

So how do you know if you are suffering from WW? Just put a check next to any of the following symptoms that describe how you're feeling now that you've reached the final stage of your Bridal Therapy voyage. If you find yourself checking one or more, it's official — WW has taken hold of your fragile frame:

☐ You have become emotionally detached or disinterested in everyday activities that used to bring you joy, like zipping up your bridesmaid dress on the svelte body you worked so hard to tone.

☐ You repeatedly peer out your front door, waiting for the mailman to deliver yet another wedding invite.

☐ You persistently avoid contact with wedding-related stimuli, such as changing the channel when J. Lo's *The Wedding Planner* comes on or crossing the street to avoid walking by the bridal dress shop downtown.

☐ You do just the opposite. You persistently fixate on wedding-related stimuli, such as alphabetizing your stockpile of wedding invitations and color-coding your massive bridesmaid dress collection.

☐ You have frequent panicked thoughts clouding your head of how to fill your now empty days

☐ You are not able to recall or discuss parts of the event, such as what happened the day of the last wedding or what made you know your wedding days were over.

☐ You experience impairment in social functioning, such as choosing not to join your now-married friends for their rare night out on the town.

Once you've diagnosed yourself with WW, you're ready to treat it. Read on to learn about the right remedy.

Your PBT Says: Overcome WW—and Quick!

No more weddings on the horizon. Check! Diagnosed with WW. Double Check! Ready to conquer WW. Triple Check!

So what's your treatment program? Detoxify your mind, body, and spirit. It's time to get down with Wedding Day Rehab.

Try this no-sweat Wedding Day Rehab Program: Five Steps to a Withdrawal-Free, Wonderful You.

1. Remove all wedding paraphernalia from your home. That's right, donate your bridesmaid dresses to charities like The Glass Slipper Project, which accepts formal dresses for in-need girls heading to the prom. Sell your silver Stuart Weitzman heels you bought for last weekend's wedding. And please, trash the unnecessarily cheesy wedding favors, like the "True Love Forever" picture frame from the Ft. Lauderdale affair or the autographed beer cozy from that Vermont wedding.

2. Lock away the wedding invites. If you're not the sentimental type, just toss 'em. If you are, you may want to look back on this crazy time in your life, so put them somewhere safe where you won't see them for the next six months.

3. Remove from your "favorites list" weddingchannel.com, macys.com, and potterybarn.com and delete any other site that even *mentions* bridal gifts.

4. Change the channel when any of the following shows up on TiVo: *Bridezillas*, *My Best Friend's Wedding*, or *27 Dresses*. The same goes for those irresistible pics of that hot celebrity couple getting hitched in *People* or *InStyle Weddings*. Toss 'em!

5. Dress down. Now that you don't have to squeeze into another cocktail dress this weekend, get reacquainted with your most comfy pair of Seven jeans and your favorite hoodie. You know, that cute gray one that hasn't seen the light of day in a couple of years. The mere fact that you're in denim and wool—and not in taffeta and toile—will help.

These simple steps will help make WW as short and pain-free as possible.

Your PBT Says: Reclaim Your Most Important Asset—You

Now that you've overcome wicked WW, you're ready for the most challenging part of Stage IX: embracing—well, you!

That's right! It may seem scary finally to focus on little old you. After all, you've been spending so much time thinking about your bride, agonizing over her needs, and catering to her every whim, you've likely forgotten about yourself a bit.

To bring things back to where they belong—with you as the center of your world—it's time to get a bit philosophical. Start by asking yourself, "Who am I?" A bridesmaid? A friend of the bride? Who else?

If you can't easily answer with' something unrelated to your bride, complete this critical step. Practice the following "Who Am I? Exercise." Just finish off each sentence with the first thing that pops into your head:

I am _____.

As a child I was _____.

As an adult I am _____.

My friends describe me as _____.

My parents describe me as _____.

I describe myself as _____.

Now that you've completed this exercise, it's clear. There's far more to you than gift giver and train buster. You're a supercute, superfun, supersmart Chiquita. And don't let anyone—or any bride—have you thinking otherwise! Go back to this exercise whenever you're feeling a bit lost about life in the non-wedding world. Feel free to give yourself a refresher on who you are and how important your life is beyond the aisle.

Your PBT Says: Embrace Your Wedding-Free World

Sure, life without guaranteed plans every Saturday night can be tough to get used to. Not getting dressed up every weekend as you prepare to walk your bride down the aisle can be challenging.

And, yes, dealing with the fact that your little sister has now moved on from wedding bells to baby planning. Well, that one may take a very long time to cope with!

But look on the bright side. You've finally gotten your freedom back. No more awkwardly fitting bridesmaid dresses with oversized cups. No more forced smiles when the BTB tells you, "I've met the one!" No more been-there-done-that games to play at wedding showers.

It's your life and you're finally taking it back!

Your PBT Says: Take It from Freud, Spend Some Time *Kid*ding Around!

Once you're set to embrace your new, Bridezilla-free life, it's time to fill the time with something. But, in Stage IX, no ordinary activities will do.

That's right. This prescription calls only—and I mean only—for activities inspired by your childhood.

"What psychological mumbo jumbo are you talking about now, PBT?" you must be wondering. Fair question!

Let me explain. Your PBT is taking yet another critical cue from the shrink bar none, Sigmund. You see, Freud believed that the key to unlocking our happiness *today* comes from understanding our experiences as children from *yesterday*.

Think about it. Sometimes the most adult-like thing to do is—well—behave like children. To remember what *really* made you happy and what *truly* made you smile. To strive for only one goal: have as much fun as possible.

Today as a woman free from the shackles of your bride, it is time to embrace this goal yet again: to remove the high heels that make it impossible to run freely, to drop the phone calls that make it impossible to think, to throw away the BlackBerry that makes it impossible to relax.

It's Time to Try Out the "Childhood Memories Trick"

Ask yourself, "What did I enjoy most as a child?" Was it rock climbing or finger painting or photography or tap dancing or gymnastics?

Stop and really take a few minutes to think about it. Use the following space provided to write down your three favorite hobbies from childhood. After you've finished, go back to your list and write down how you can take on each hobby in today's real-life, grown-up world. For instance, if your favorite childhood hobby was fishing with your dad, one way to reapply the same idea today is to take a sushi class with your best friend.

♦ Favorite childhood hobby 1: _____
How can I incorporate this fun into my life today?

_____

_____

♦ Favorite childhood hobby 2: _____
How can I incorporate this fun into my life today?

_____

_____

♦ Favorite childhood hobby 3: _____
How can I incorporate this fun into my life today?

_____

_____

Your PBT Says: Congratulations—for Now!

Whew! You've made it through nearly all nine stages of the horrid wedding process! You've even identified ways to spend your bride-free time.

Go ahead and pat yourself on the back—you deserve it. But, don't let your bride out of your sights for long. Stage IX ain't over yet. Just as soon as you have a minute to yourself, she'll reappear, this time with a new bag of tricks.

Your PBT Says: Meet Your New Best Friend, the Married Lady

Your bride's wedding ring was one thing. Her eternal vows of commitment were another. And now your bride expects you to deal easily with her as a married woman! To embrace her un-single life!

"No way!" you'll say. You've completed your job as bridesmaid or MOH or best friend of the bride. "Why am I now being asked to do more?"

Great question, my adorableness. The unfortunate answer? Unless you're ready to sever your friendship, give back the other half of your BFF necklace, or declare your self "estranged" from your sister, it's time for you to cope with what nearly every Bridezilla becomes: a real live "Married Lady."

"But, wait a minute!" you say. "I thought that term was only reserved for people like my mom or my forty-eight-year-old boss."

"Since when is my BFF/sister/cousin a Christmas-sweater-wearing slouch?" "Since when does she care about heating up dinners and preparing the house for company?" "Since when do microwave models and baby books fit into your daily conversations?"

You guessed it. Since she said, "I do."

That's right. Just because you've done your duty as best friend or bridesmaid, putting up with nearly every request your Bridezilla demanded, doesn't mean your job is over. And it certainly doesn't mean life will return to normal. In fact, life will never be the same again.

Prepare yourself for those dreaded words, "I'm a married lady now."

She'll likely use this phrase for the first shocking time when you're out for drinks a couple months after the wedding, as the clock strikes a measly 9:30 P.M. or when she declines your "Girls' Night Out Dinner" evite.

You will be left wondering, "What's worse? The fact that she's left you to be married or that she actually used the term, 'lady,' to describe herself? After all, she's married. But she's not fifty!"

Either way, get ready for the Married Lady that will surely come knockin' on your door.

How do you know if you're dealing with one? Read on.

The Top Ten Signs That She's Officially a Married Lady Now

10. She cut her hair a la Katie Holmes.

9. She talks about how great her company is at allowing women to work from home or take time off for kids.

8. She's just bought her first pair of tapered, mom-like jeans.

7. She uses the word "baby" more than once in your conversation.

6. She spends her Saturdays shopping for a new Tudor house instead of shopping for a new pair of suede boots.

5. She's gained at least five pounds since the wedding.

4. She now has conversations consisting of home decorating tips instead of picking-up-men tips.

3. She answers the phone when you call her at 8:30 P.M. on Saturday night, and you're guaranteed to find her on the couch.

2. She's traded her cute, yellow VW bug from college for a minivan.

1. She suddenly becomes shy when the waiter tries to flirt with your once normally flirtatious friend while at dinner.

Read on about Ricki R. to understand what's in store for you next.

Bridal Case File #14: **Ricki R.**

Ricki R. describes the precise moment she knew that her best friend became a Married Lady with one word: traumatic.

"I couldn't believe my ears or my eyes," Ricki R. vented, as she explained her first night out with her closest friend since the wedding. "She was an entirely different person— virtually overnight."

The two friends were inseparable; as teachers at a snooty preschool in Connecticut, they had to deal not only with the snobby kids but, worse, with their stay-at-home, nothing-else-to-do-but-worry-about-their-kids moms.

The wedding prep and the wedding, itself, were great. In fact, Ricki R.'s bride was anything but a Bridezilla, and the wedding was anything but boring. Ricki R. had a great time at the wedding, even scoring her own wedding-night-only hook up.

When Ricki R.'s bride called the day after her honeymoon adventure in Cabo, Ricki R. couldn't wait to see her. When the bride suggested that they meet for civilized coffee—as opposed to the somewhat uncivilized cabernets the two would usually down—Ricki R. didn't think twice.

But when she laid eyes on the typically skinny-mini, Kate Spade bag-toting, Tory Burch flat-wearing, blond-highlighted teacher, she nearly fell over. Her bride was easily fifteen pounds heavier. Her long locks had been chopped and dyed back to their natural mousy brown. And an Old Navy sweatshirt and faded Levis replaced her once high-fashion outfit.

The situation only got worse when the two women sat down over mochas. After Ricki R. went on for what she knew was too long about her wedding-night hook-up adventure, she turned the conversation back to the bride. "So, how is married life?" she asked.

"I love it. We have the best life ever!" the bride said with a smile that reminded Ricki R. of her sixty-five-year-old mother. "He goes to work. And now that I've cut my teaching schedule down to three days a week, I clean. I cook dinner. Then, he comes home."

She went on, "We eat together. We watch *ER*. Then, at about 11:00, it's time for bed."

"What was happening?" Ricki R. wondered. "Who was this creature? Did some alien-like husband snatch her away and replace her with June Cleaver?"

"I know it sounds really lame, but I actually like it," the married matron defended.

Hearing those words calmed Ricki R. down. At least her wild-child teacher could admit that things had changed. And at least she was happy.

So what lesson can you learn from Ricki R.? Be prepared for the shock you'll feel when your once party-hearty bestie suddenly shows up as a way-too-tame married matron.

Your PBT's words of advice: embrace the change. Someday you, too, may be picking out window curtain patterns and buying Dawn dish detergent by the gallon. Until that day comes, remember that change is part of any lasting friendship. So even if you can barely recognize her in her brown minivan, she's still the same friend with whom you were camp counselors together—the same friend who did everything she could to get you out of detention in fifth grade. No I'm-married-now haircut or reduced work schedule can change that.

Your PBT Says: Bridal Therapy Is Never Over!

You've officially been through it all! All the pre-wedding migraines, the wedding day nonsense, the post-wedding drama. All nine stages of the mind-boggling, confidence-shaking wedding process. And guess what? You actually lived to tell about it.

In fact, you've done far more than that. Thanks to a few tricks of the psychotherapy trade—and more importantly to your un-ending desire to take the psychological high ground—you've officially completed this Bridal Therapy Program with honors.

And just like your fourth-grade teacher awarded you with a certificate for the best haiku in the class, your PBT is equally as honored to award you with this one-of-a-kind certificate of Bridal Therapy Completion.

SHE'S GONE BRIDAL!

This certifies that

_____

has satisfactorily completed the 9 Stages
of the official
BRIDAL THERAPY PROGRAM
and is entitled to
SANITY — FRIENDSHIP —
PEACE OF MIND
AND ALL THE PRIVILEGES THAT
APPERTAIN THEREUNTO

on this _____ day of _____, 20____.

Yours truly,
Your Personal Bridal Therapist (PBT)

Go ahead. Photocopy the certificate. Write your name in the empty space. Carry it with you in your Gucci purse whenever your next bride starts to get the best of you. Hang it on your fridge as a badge of honor. Even frame it for your wall of honors, perhaps right next to your diploma from UCLA.

But remember, just because your PBT has awarded you with this cute little certificate doesn't mean your therapy is over. In fact, Bridal Therapy never truly ends. As wedding updo's come undone, as bridal showers give way to baby showers, and as your friendship with your bride evolves, you can always reapply the therapeutic lessons you learned in *She's Gone Bridal!*.

You can also use your Bridal Therapy knowledge to help others in need. Create your very own Bridal Therapy sessions; just pick a night once a month to swap stories and read advice from this book with friends, family members, or co-workers.

So whether it's Bridal Mode, Groom Mode, or even Baby Mode that you default to in your next trying situation; whether you're dealing with a bride from hell, a groom from the underworld, or a non-bridal brat, always remember, keep your head up, flash your pearly whites, and make *you* the top priority on your list—no matter whose name is on the wedding invitation!

Yours truly,
Your Personal Bridal Therapist (PBT)

Emergency Services

*Surefire tips for even the worst-case scenario
Bridezilla situations*

> *Stomping feet.*
> *Flashing lights.*
> *Frantic crowds.*
> *"Get me out of here!" you yell.*
> *Not to fear — it's just a wedding, my dear!*

Sure. These sights and sounds are all signals you would normally equate with a real-life emergency. But did you know that they also emerge at many a matrimonial affair?

Emergency situations, along with words like "stat" and "intervention," are no longer solely reserved for shows like *Grey's Anatomy*. These days, brides are causing emergencies of their own — some that rival even the most heart-wrenching situations on *ER* — every day. In the end, innocent victims — like you — are left alarmed, unnerved, and helpless.

That's where your very own PBT comes in, yet again! This section of *She's Gone Bridal!* dives deep into some of the bridal emergency situations you may encounter. And, of course, your

PBT advises you on how to handle every one with the grace and poise that you've mastered throughout your wedding odyssey. Just think of this section as a Bridal Crisis Center—Bridal 9-1-1 if you will—for any and every wedding emergency. And remember, whenever you're ready to declare a state of wedding emergency, this PBT will be right there with you to sound the alarm!

Your PBT Says: Learn Bridal Emergency Protocol

According to experts at the American Red Cross, there is a very specific protocol for coping with emergency situations. Sure, these rules were designed for tricky situations like earthquakes and landslides. But that hasn't stopped your PBT—forever devoted to making your bridal life better—from reapplying them to your bridal situation. Besides, when it comes to your bride, it sure does feel as if she's had a disaster-like impact on your life!

Take a few minutes to study the three phases required to cope with any bridal emergency:

Phase I: Bridal Preparedness

The best way to cope with any emergency—real life or bridal life—is to be prepared. That's why you should always be ready and thinking ahead about what could possibly go wrong at any given moment. Sure, it may seem a bit negative, but you always want to ask yourself, "What is the worst thing that could happen right now?"

For example, if your bride is going for her final fitting, ask yourself, "What is the worst thing that could happen now?" You might imagine that the seamstress could rip the dress or that the bride could have gained seven pounds. That's the kind of thinking you need to get into your cute little head.

Bridal Case File #46: Casey F.

Casey F.'s bridal emergency is an excellent example of how preparedness can turn around any disaster—no matter how torrential.

Casey F.'s bride—and even Casey F. herself—were stoked about the beautiful location for the wedding: an outdoor ceremony at the local botanical gardens in Atlanta. The forecast had been simply perfect: sunny with a few clouds for the entire day. Casey F. and the bride thought they had it made! In fact, the day before the wedding, they conducted the rehearsal outside and looked forward to the next, rain-free day.

When Casey F. awoke to the sound of thunder, torrential rain, and high winds in the middle of the night, however, she knew immediately that this storm would threaten the next day's celebration. And as any well-trained woman would do in this situation, Casey F. had a plan to tackle the storm head-on.

Before heading over to the bride's suite the next morning, Casey F. drove—in the rain—to the nearest Target, scoured the shelves, and picked up six pairs of the cutest galoshes and matching umbrellas you've ever seen. She knew these would look adorable on the bridal party. She also bought twenty pink umbrellas for the guests.

When Casey F. arrived at the bridal suite, she had saved the day. And when the bridal party walked down the aisle in the slippery garden with their supersweet, shloshey shoes and umbrellas, the wedding disaster magically transformed into a wedding success.

Casey F. not only helped out her bride but kept the cutest pair of galoshes for herself that she *still* wears when the weather permits!

Phase II: Bridal Response and Recovery

Borrowing again from the Red Cross, you know that after an emergency occurs, the first thing you need to do is obvious: respond. But the *best* way to respond is not quite as obvious. You need to stay as calm and even-keeled as possible. No matter how "ginormous" the run in the bride's panty hose, no matter how many times your fellow bridesmaid pukes in the country club bathroom, and no matter how many tears the groom—yes, the groom—cries, it is up to you to shrug your shoulders, smile, and respond as unphased as possible.

In Lucy R.'s case, her unruffable personality was perfect for Phase II. Dealing constantly with the high drama of B-list directors and photographers, this LA production assistant knew how to remain calm no matter how much swirl surrounded her.

When it came time for her own mother's wedding in San Diego, Lucy R. simply imagined that her mom was a high-maintenance director and that she was her cool-as-a-cucumber right-hand woman—never flinching, no matter how big her mother's bridal emergency got.

So take a cue from Lucy R.! After all, when the wedding world goes crazy, why should you enter the loony bin? Stay cool not only for your bride—but, more importantly, for yourself.

Phase III: Bridal Mitigation

Once the situation has been resolved, it is up to you—again—to take the reins. In this phase, your role is to take the required steps to ensure that the emergency does not repeat itself.

If your bride gets completely sloshed during the rehearsal dinner, for example, do whatever you can to ensure that she doesn't get her hands on that martini the night of the wedding.

Also, if you notice that the bride's cousin Vincent keeps slipping his hand on your thigh the night of the engagement party, for instance, you surely do not want a repeat performance of this inappropriate behavior. Do whatever you need to do to stay clear of this guy—even if it means convincing your guy friend to play "boyfriend" for the night.

Your PBT Says: Abide by These Basic Principles

In addition to sticking to required bridal protocol, it is critical that you remember a few principles when dealing with your bridal emergency—no matter how devastating the situation.

Principle 1: Chose your words carefully.

Avoid catastrophic language that can make the situation seem worse than it truly is. For example, when your bride decides that she's no longer interested in marrying her adorable fiancé—a clear bridal emergency situation—be sure not to describe the situation as "a tragedy" or "the worst day ever."

That's right. No matter how disastrous the situation may *seem*, ask yourself: "Is there some way to remedy the situation?" "Is this really the end of the world?"

The day that stone-washed jeans come back—now that's the end of the world, not this. And it is often up to you to keep the situation in perspective and under control.

Read on about Melanie P. and about how her choiceful words at her friend's wedding saved the day.

Bridal Case File #18: Melanie P.

There was only one word fitting of Melanie P.'s bride, whom she had known since culinary school in San Fran: foodie. So when it came time for her friend's wedding, Melanie P. knew the food would be the absolute best part of the event.

BONUS THERAPY: EMERGENCY SERVICES

From the wonderful wine at the start of the evening to the fantastic filet at dinner, the evening was a night of food, food, and more food.

That was until it came time for the cake. Melanie P.'s bride, now a pastry chef in LA, had created the most divine cake in the entire valley. As the bride and groom set out to cut the cake, the bride held her one-year-old daughter in her arms for the photo. When she began to cut the symbolic first slice, her seemingly angelic daughter kicked her foot into the cake, cracking the lacey frosting and cutting a Mary Jane line directly through to the lemon meringue filling.

For a foodie, it was a full-on food disaster!

Melanie P. rushed to her bride's side, grabbed her daughter out of her arms and—as the bride began to shed a tear for her now lopsided cake—Melanie P. reminded her of a lesson from their favorite chef at culinary school, "Never cry over spilled milk," she told her friend.

With that, the bride turned her tear of panic into resolve and went with it—with a smile. The two removed a tier from the cake and served the rest to the amused guests.

Principle 2: Laugh it up!

No matter how coordinated the bridesmaid dresses, no matter how intricate the table settings, no matter how precise the directions to the church, weddings are bound to go wrong somewhere.

At some point, the wrong fabric will be ordered, the vegetarian entrée will be served to the carnivore, the bridesmaid will walk down the aisle too quickly, and the wrong name will sometimes be uttered during the vows. But, hey, that's wedding life.

It's up to you to do all you can to stay attuned to—and ready to laugh at—each of these potential emergencies. Remember, if your bride has even the smallest ounce of humanity left in her, she'll remember to crack a smile herself and enjoy what she came there to do: get hitched.

Read on about how Cindy R. found a way to bring humor to her bride—and herself.

Bridal Case File #23: Cindy R.

Cindy R.'s bride was not your typical Bridezilla. Sure, she was demanding. Sure, she was a perfectionist. Sure, she obsessed over every detail of the big day.

But what separated Cindy R.'s bride from the rest of the Bridezilla pack was her great sense of humor. No matter how bleak the situation, this bride was always able to crack a joke to make herself—and those around her—feel better.

So on the day of her autumn wedding, this humor was put to the ultimate test when the florist decided simply not to show up. After awaiting his arrival for nearly four hours and frantically phoning him umpteen times, Cindy R. came to the realization that this flower had officially wilted.

Thanks to Cindy R., however, the reception would still be filled with natural beauty. Cindy R. phoned a few of the folks who she knew would be attending the wedding and sent them out on a critical mission: buy as many pumpkins in as many shapes and sizes as possible. In less than two hours, Cindy R. had two dozen pumpkins and gourds at her fingertips.

Working with the five other bridesmaids, she lined the aisle with the roundest pumpkins and turned the cutest gourds into centerpieces with hand-painted table numbers.

When the bride first laid eyes on Cindy R.'s creation, she let out a laugh of joy and relief. In the end, the wedding emergency was diverted and the wedding was perfectly seasonal!

Principle 3: Remember, there's only so much you can do.

That's right. No matter how perfect a bridesmaid you pride yourself on being, and no matter how great a BFF you are, oftentimes there is only so much even *you* can do.

When the band doesn't show up, when the MOB hits on a young groomsman, and when the groom gets it on with the housekeeper the night before the wedding, there's simply too much potential for something to go wrong.

So remember, sometimes there are situations that you simply can't do more than hope that someday—whether it's tomorrow or two years from now—you can look back on with some much-needed perspective.

Your PBT Says: Learn How to Handle *Any* Bridal Situation

Now that you've learned the critical principles to handle bridal emergencies, it is time to put them into practice with real-world, real-life examples of bridal emergencies. As a special therapy treat, some of my most prized patients helped me craft a series of "must know" questions and answers about how to tackle the worst-case scenario bridal emergency situations. Just think of this as your PBT's "Dear Abby" for your wedding worriment.

When She Jokes About Calling It Off—Get Serious

Dear PBT,

My bride threatened several times to call off her upcoming wedding. At first, she mentioned this idea as a joke in passing. But as the wedding date approaches—now only two months away—she has become more serious about these threats. What do I do, PBT?

> Not laughing anymore in Colorado,
> Lexi K.

Dear Lexi K.,

Well, this certainly qualifies as a true bridal emergency! It's one thing to make a joke about not wanting to tie the knot. It's another to make serious statements about it. If your bride is really talking about calling off the wedding, you need to take her threats seriously.

Probe, but not too hard. If she, indeed, really feels as if getting married now would be wrong, remind her that the most important thing is not the invitations or the presents or the gifts, but rather whether she wants to be with this man for the rest of her life. Your role is to help her remember what is important in the situation and to help her make the best decision for her.

So no matter how you feel about her fiancé, don't focus on telling her what to do, but rather on helping her come to the right decision on her own.

> Yours truly,
> Your Personal Bridal Therapist (PBT)

When the Dress Just Doesn't Fit, Do As Tim Gunn Does and "Make It Work"

Dear PBT,

I have gained a few pounds since I placed the order for my icky bridesmaid dress. Now that the holidays have ended and I've practically eaten my way through the fridge, the dress just doesn't fit. I've got three months till the wedding. What should I do?

> Desperately trying to make it work in Wisconsin,
> Candice E.

Dear Candice E.,

It's officially time to begin your Wedding Day Detox! Just follow these three suggestions, and you'll be able to squeeze right into your fancy frock.

Tip 1: Drink eight glasses of water every day. Sure, this may have you running to the bathroom during work meetings, but more importantly, it'll help your body get rid of all the extra stuff you don't want.

Tip 2: Replace half of your plate with a serving of fresh veggies at every meal.

Tip 3: "Up" the exercise factor by adding thirty minutes to your daily workout where you need it most. If it's your waist, go for some belly dancing classes. If it's your arms, try some push-ups. If it's your legs, try some dance lessons with that cute Russian instructor you spotted in the window at Debbie's School of Dance downtown.

> Yours truly,
> Your Personal Bridal Therapist (PBT)

When Your Date Cancels, Make the Most of a Single Girl's Night Out

Dear PBT,

I was superexcited to attend my BFF's Napa Valley destination wedding with my new supercute man. It was my first chance to show him off to my college friends. At the last minute, however, he suddenly had to attend a work function. What's a now dateless girl to do?

Dateless in Dakota,
Alicia D.

Dear Alicia D.,

Not to fret, my friend! There are a few ways to handle the situation. One is to get a date last minute. Ask your best guy friend or co-worker. Who wouldn't want to accompany a cutie-pie like you? Then, treat the wedding as if it were a fun night out on the town. Lucky for you, you'll look your best, drink free alcohol, and have an excuse to ask for a dance.

Yours truly,
Your Personal Bridal Therapist (PBT)

When Your Bride Is a Certified Lush, Tread with Caution

Dear PBT,

I've noticed that my bride gets seriously drunk—I'm talking about falling over on her face—at all her wedding events, from the engagement party to the wedding shower to the bachelorette party. Sipping a few Cosmos is surely to be expected for my sorority sister party girl, but I wonder if she has a drinking problem. How can I help?

> Wasted with Worry in Michigan,
> Sandra F.

Dear Sandra F.,

Your instincts are probably right. If you believe your bride is too drunk for her own good far too many a time, you are indeed facing a bridal emergency. Unfortunately, there is only so much you can do today.

Your PBT recommends that you sit down with your bride during a nonalcohol-infused lunch or coffee break to discuss your concern. If she seems amenable and open, discuss ways she can cut down on the drinks.

If she seems angry and not open to your advice, put on the breaks! Given how stressed and anxious she likely is, the time right before her wedding is likely not the best to tackle this potential drinking issue. Wait until the wedding is over to rehash the topic.

Either way, remind her that she needs to attend the wedding in a fully conscious state!

> Yours truly,
> Your Personal Bridal Therapist (PBT)

When the Wedding Music Sucks, Embrace It

Dear PBT,

I recently attended my co-worker's wedding. All I can say is, the wedding band was a big, hot mess! Not only were the selections cheesy and out of tune, but the crowd was so uninspired that no one danced. In fact, many of the guests just spent time sitting in their chairs talking about how badly they wanted to hear the new JT single. What could I have done in this situation?

> Yearning for Justin in Massachusetts,
> Monica B.

Dear Monica B.,

In this case, your bridal behavior was unacceptable. You were witness to a real-life wedding emergency and stood idly by. When faced with a situation like this in the future, your first recourse is to embrace the cheese. No matter how bad the music, get out there and dance, dance, dance!

After all, you spent all that time and money getting all dolled up—you might as well enjoy yourself. And besides, what better excuse to dance with that cutie at your table? Simply ask him, "Want to dance to this dreadful music with me?" How can he say no?

In addition, you owe it to yourself and to all the other miserable guests at the reception to attempt to remedy the situation. Simply go up to the band or DJ and ask for your favorite Madonna or Brit-Brit song. The DJ's guaranteed to make you—and the rest of the unlucky wedding party—more inspired to dance than they were before.

> Yours truly,
> Your Personal Bridal Therapist (PBT)

When There's a Stain on the Dress, Don't Distress

Dear PBT,

I recently received the bridesmaid dress for my little cousin's wedding. Luckily, I ordered the dress several months in advance of the wedding. Unluckily, however, as I was transporting the dress from the bridal shop to my downtown

Dallas apartment, the sunny weather suddenly turned into a torrential downpour. The dress and I made it home safe and sound with the exception of a tiny rain stain near the hem.

The stain doesn't really bother me, but I know my detail-obsessed bride will surely notice. What is a Southern girl to do?

Stained in the South,
Dori R.

Dear Dori R.,

Quite the bridal emergency, indeed! It doesn't get much worse than dealing with bridesmaid dress disasters.

The first question for you to answer: Can your dry cleaner fix the stain? Head over to the best dry cleaner in Dallas, even if it means spending a few extra bucks. Bat your Southern belle eyelashes and ask him what he can do to help. These days, most dry-cleaning experts are able to work more magic than you can conjure up.

Next, if your Texan dry cleaner is not able to help, you may be able to order another dress in time for the wedding. Go directly to the store where you purchased the gown. Explain the situation and ask how quickly they can order and ship the dress to you. If it will arrive in a minimum of two weeks before the wedding day, that gives you enough time to receive it, have it tailored, and wear it in all its bridesmaid glory. Be forewarned, of course: ordering this last minute may mean additional charges, but the price will likely be worth it.

Last, once you've exhausted all options, ask your fellow bridesmaids to save any extra fabric from their alterations. You can always ask your seamstress to replace the stained area on your hem with a nice, clean piece from one of your fellow bridesmaid's scraps.

Yours truly,
Your Personal Bridal Therapist (PBT)

When Hair and Makeup Cancel, Stay Calm

Dear PBT,

It's just two weeks before my BFF's super-glam wedding in Beverly Hills, and the most unglam thing is wreaking havoc on the entire bridal party including me—the MOH! The bride's celebrity-like hair maven cancelled at the last minute, explaining that his admin accidentally double-booked him for another wedding at the same time. How can I save the bride's hair—and more importantly, my own?

Waiting to be Coiffed in California,
Samantha V.

Dear Samantha V.,

This is a very common wedding emergency—and there's no question about it—when it comes to hair, any change in plans surely qualifies as a true emergency. There are a few courses of action for you, my hair-challenged cherie.

First, ask this hair "guru" if there is anyone else at his salon who can take his place. This is the least he can do. Unfortunately, if he's not that dependable, it may be hard to trust someone else from his salon. But he should be able to do this for you and the bridal party at the very least.

Next, search for other cancellations. Very often, when one bride cancels, appointments open up. In this instance, there are bound to be some last-minute cancellations, even for Cali's high-end clientele.

Check the phone book. Call the top ten salons in the city. Reserve whomever you can for the big day.

Last, scour local beauty schools. This may sound a bit desperate, but there is a ton of hidden talent, especially in towns as beauty conscious as LA. Take out a want ad, put up posters in the local salon. Do whatever it takes to get someone who can decently put your and the bridal party's hair into the buns you so deserve.

Yours truly,
Your Personal Bridal Therapist (PBT)

Your PBT Says: Master the Art of Bridal Intervention

Now that you've learned to cope with nearly every real-life bridal emergency, you need to prepare yourself for the wedding disaster to end all disasters—the Bridezilla gone bad.

In this situation, we're not talking about the usually manageable bridal behavior you've learned how to deal with. We're talking about a different breed—a Bridezilla who has gone too far, victimizing you in her path.

In this rare but troubling case, the only solution to curtail her behavior and improve your life is a full-on Bridal Intervention.

"Just what is a Bridal Intervention?" you ask.

Well, my jewel, in the real world an intervention is an event in which a group of people confront another to help that person address serious personal problems, such as alcoholism or drug abuse.

A Bridal Intervention works the same way. Instead of confronting someone about her drug or alcohol problem, you and others close to her confront the bride about her thoughtless Bride-zilla behavior.

But before you resort to such a drastic measure, it's critical to determine whether it's time for a Bridal Intervention. Take the following quick diagnostic quiz.

"Am I Ready for a Bridal Intervention?" Quiz

Sign 1: The bride quit her job to focus on wedding planning.

Sign 2: The bride has caused everyone who knows her—from her BFFs to her co-workers to her grandmother—to be disturbed by her bad behavior.

Sign 3: The bride has so disgusted her groom with her attitude that he's confused and thinking of postponing—or cancelling—the wedding.

Sign 4: The bride refers to herself in the third person as "the bride."

Sign 5: The bride talks about the future, but she doesn't get past May 22nd, the day of the wedding.

Sign 6: The bride made you cry. More than once.

If your bride exhibits two or more of the symptoms just described, it's official—the only way to cope is with a true Bridal Intervention.

Next, determine who should join you for the intervention meeting. Ask yourself, "Are there other people, like a fellow bridesmaid or friend, who have experienced the same issues?" "Is there someone in particular who knows the bride very well and whom the bride would respond to?"

Next, work with your Bridal Intervention buddies to plan out exactly what you will say to the bride. Think about ways to be as positive as possible, explaining to the bride not only what she's doing wrong, but what she's doing right. Offer suggestions for how to improve her behavior.

For example, if your bride seemed ungrateful for all the hard work you put into her wedding shower, make sure you not only tell her how this made you feel but also be sure to add an example of a situation in which she made you feel great. That way, she can model her behavior after something positive.

If your bad, bad Bridezilla's got any heart—or brain—left in her, she'll likely respond to your Bridal Intervention. And that means a better bridal existence for you in no time!

Speedy Bridal Therapy

In five minutes or less

Sure, you memorized each and every tactic in your Bridal Therapy Program. You mastered the art of Bridal Mode. You even caught yourself passing along some therapeutic advice of your own to fellow victims of the bride. You overachiever, you! But even the most prized pupil, like yourself, needs a quick bridal pick-me-up every once in a while. That's what this Bonus Therapy section is for!

For those of you in a mad dash to deal with your diva-like bride, have no fear. Your kind-hearted PBT is here, sprinting right alongside you! So whether you need a swift Bridal Therapy refresher as you're heading out the door to your cube mate's bridal shower or determining the right gift to purchase from Williams-Sonoma's registry for your college roommate's wedding, take a read. Pronto!

- *Stage I: Denial:* When she announces her engagement, you'll likely be in denial that she is actually leaving you—and your "single-girl" life together—to become a bride. What's the secret to your bridal success? Putting into practice your Bridal Mode skills: just stay cool, calm, and collected and you'll turn denial into acceptance in no time flat.

- *Stage II: Diagnosis:* Once you've accepted that she's actually a BTB, it's time to diagnose her with the appropriate bridal personality, whether it's the Indecisive Bride or the Control Freak Bride. And once you've accurately diagnosed her, you'll be ready to tailor your therapeutic responses precisely to her unique bridal personality and keep *your* own personality in check.

- *Stage III: Masquerading:* Now that you know what kind of bride you're dealing with, you'll need to assume the role of good friend throughout the process. From the engagement party to the wedding shower to the big day itself, the key to keeping your friendship intact? Remember that her bridal behavior is only temporary and that you'll likely look back on her nightmarish wedding ten years from now and laugh. Or at least manage to smile!

- *Stage IV: Anger:* Whether you're frustrated about giving up your weekend to go wedding dress shopping or resentful that she's landed the man—and ring—of your dreams, you'll probably feel slighted during this stage. But taking a moment to acknowledge your mixed feeling about your bestie's matrimony will help you get through this phase. Fast.

- *Stage V: Transference:* Once you've dealt with your negative feelings about the bride, you'll want to spend some time indulging in the bridal "good life." And surely there's no shame in "transferring" the benefits of being a bride over to you. Just be sure not to forget the champagne toast to your own "unwedded" bliss!

- *Stage VI: Fixation:* As your bridal journey continues on, it's easy to become obsessed with your bride's wedding. So much so, that you forget to take care of the most important person in the process—you. Remember, it may be her wedding, but it is *your* life. No matter how big her wedding gets, you need to retain—or regain—your sense of self.

- *Stage VII: Family therapy:* In addition to remembering to take care of yourself, you'll need to take on several family members and friends who put even the worst bride to shame, like the Mom-Zilla or the Groom from Hell. How do you manage this monstrous group of misfits? Just reapply Bridal Mode and you're golden!

- *Stage VIII: Catharsis:* When the wedding day finally arrives, all your energy, anxiety, and frustration will finally come to a wonderful moment of joy and freedom. Take a moment to relish the thrill of the "I do's" finally being done.

- *Stage IX: Withdrawal:* Now that the weddings have ended and there are no more invitations on the horizon, you'll finally be able to take a bride-free deep breath. But don't be surprised if panic and sadness set in as your life without your bride feels empty and boring. What's your covert coping mechanism? Focus on finding ways to refocus on yourself again.

Overcoming the Punch
of Pregnancy News

First comes love. Well, sometimes.
Then, comes marriage. Um, usually.
Then comes a baby in a baby carriage. Definitely!
Brace yourself.

Once you've gotten through the wedding whirlwind, it's time for another shock to your well-trained system. It's got four letters and an infinite impact: B-A-B-Y.

Once you've wrapped your cute headband-adorned little head around the fact that your once-single bride is living the life you never imagined she would—as a happily married woman—she'll shock you once again with the news that she's having a baby.

And that's exactly how it may seem. One day she's the hour-glass-figured friend you secretly envy—the next day she's wad-dling around in Gap maternity clothes. And the next, out pops cute little Chloe Savannah already wearing designer jeans and baby UGGs.

So sit down for this one. Strap on your safety belt 'cause there ain't no stopping this baby train from getting to the station. Get yourself—and your penchant for binkees and receiving blankets—ready. It's baby time!

The secret to coping with your bride's newfound obsessions—conceiving, delivering, and raising a baby? You guessed it! It's

"Baby Mode." That's right. Just as you converted your best Bridal Mode skills to Groom Mode, now you'll be a whiz at switching them to Baby Mode. Same pain for you. Different situation for her.

Just imagine it. When she starts talking about baby names or about taking time off from work or about the cutest maternity leggings, simply do what you're trained to do. Smile hard. Hug tight. Even throw your arms up and shout, "I can't wait for the cutest baby ever!"

By now, this should really come as second nature to someone as well prepared and experienced as you.

This time, the wedding event and all the preparation for the big day is replaced by an actual human. I know, I know. This is pretty heavy stuff but not as (beautifully!) heavy as she's guaranteed to be at month seven!

To begin to comprehend this Huggies-filled phase, learn from Kaitlyn S., below.

Bridal Case File #37: Kaitlyn S.

When the phone rang at 7:30 P.M. on that infamous St. Patty's Tuesday night, Kaitlyn S. knew from the "When the Saints Come Marching In" ringtone who it was—and why she was calling—without even looking at the phone. The personalized ringtone meant it was her best friend calling. But it was pure instinct that led Kaitlyn S. to know—without a doubt—why her former college roommate was calling.

The two once very close friends hadn't spoken in about three months—which was average for the girls since they now lived on two opposite ends of the country. The last time they spoke, Kaitlyn S.'s now married bride had told her over drinks, "Now that I've finished grad school and Mark is so established at Google, there's really no reason to wait any longer."

"Wait for what?" Kaitlyn S. asked and then quickly gulped down another glass.

"A baby—of course!" her friend laughed as she told her. "Of course!"

Skip ahead to the leprechaun-filled celebration. Alas, the day had arrived. And as Kaitlyn S. prepared herself to hear the news—that the first of her friends from college would actually be giving birth to one of those little things called a baby—Kaitlyn S. said out loud before even answering the phone, "She's calling to tell me she's pregnant!"

Sure enough! Kaitlyn S. was absolutely correct. When she answered the phone, all it took was ten seconds. "Hi Kat!," her friend began. Without waiting for a "hello" back, she went in for the kill, "I am pregnant!"

With those three little words, Kaitlyn S.'s reality changed dramatically. The same person she used to call at 4:00 A.M. with a boy crisis had become a pregnant woman. The same person with whom she used to shop for going-out "boobie shirts" had become a responsible mom to be. The same person with whom she received a St. Louis University Police "warning" because of the pair's rambunctious behavior was now sporting a growing belly.

Immediately, Kaitlyn S. sprang into Baby Mode.

Today the baby is happy and cooing. In fact, Kaitlyn S. visited the little ball of a baby over Christmas. After having nine months to let it sink in, it was still a shock to see her college friend as a doting mom. She was breast-feeding, carriage strolling, and Gerber "choo-choo train" feeding.

But Kaitlyn S. used Baby Mode like the best of 'em.

And now that two more of her college friends are preg-
gers, she's getting more practice than she thought of Baby
Mode!

What can you learn from Kaitlyn S.? Just as soon as you've
recovered from the bridal tidal wave, the baby boom is soon to
crash on your shore!

Sources

en.wikipedia.org/wiki/Denial

www.psyskills.com/cogther01.htm

www.cedu.niu.edu/~shumow/itt/Anger%20Management.pdf

www.thebridalbook.com/archive/fall2005/jealousbride.html

en.wikipedia.org/wiki/Jealousy

www.lifescript.com/channels/well_being/meditations_
motivations/when_jealousy_rears_its_ugly_head.asp

en.wikipedia.org/wiki/Transference

en.wikipedia.org/wiki/Obsessive-compulsive_disorder

en.wikipedia.org/wiki/Individuation

www.wedalert.com/content/planning/calendar.asp

en.wikipedia.org/wiki/Salvador_Minuchin

en.wikipedia.org/wiki/Family_therapy

en.wikipedia.org/wiki/Catharsis

en.wikipedia.org/wiki/Withdrawal

en.wikipedia.org/wiki/Post-traumatic_stress_disorder

en.wikipedia.org/wiki/Special_education

www.sciencedaily.com/articles/s/special_education.htm

en.wikipedia.org/wiki/Alcoholics_Anonymous

www.drphil.com/articles/article/352

en.wikipedia.org/wiki/Intervention_%28counseling%29

SOURCES

en.wikipedia.org/wiki/Psychiatric_rehabilitation

www.ivillage.co.uk/health/hlive/style/articles/0,,181167_608089,00.html

en.wikipedia.org/wiki/Emergency

www.redcross.org/